Understanding the Chesapeake

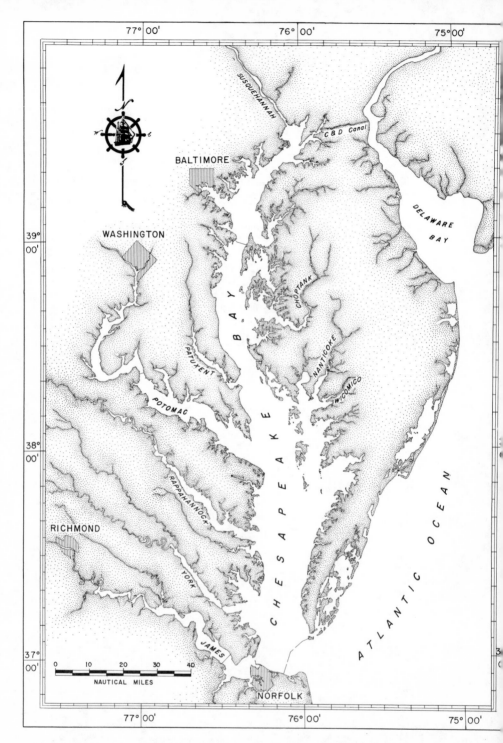

An overview of the Bay Country. Courtesy of the Chesapeake Bay Consortium.

Understanding

the

Chesapeake

A Layman's Guide

by

ARTHUR W. SHERWOOD

Director, The Chesapeake Bay Foundation, Inc.

Tidewater Publishers

Centreville   *Maryland*

Library of Congress Cataloging in Publication Data

Sherwood, Arthur W   1927-
  Understanding the Chesapeake, A layman's guide
  Bibliography;   p
  1. Marine Ecology—Chesapeake Bay
  2. Chesapeake Bay
  I. Title
QH2.5.C47S47   574.92′1′47   73-21691
ISBN 0-87033-189-2

Manufactured in the United States of America

First edition, 1973; Third printing, 1982

CONTENTS

Appendix

LIST OF ILLUSTRATIONS

PREFACE

This little book is an attempt to interpret viewpoints which, taken together, reasonably inform us of the Chesapeake Bay's peculiarities, charm, productivity, strength, and susceptibility to damage.

Eight points of view are expressed. All, naturally enough, are subject to the influence of my own experience, prejudices, and circumstances.

By training a lawyer, I am currently director of The Chesapeake Bay Foundation, Inc. (CBF), a private, nonprofit, conservation organization which operates to involve citizens in the care of the natural resources of the Chesapeake Bay region. Founded in 1964, it presently administers three programs: environmental education, emphasizing student exposure to the Bay estuarine system; representational service to citizens, including biological field work and legal aid; and preservation of natural areas acquired by the Foundation by gift. CBF Reports are published bimonthly and are mailed to members. Much of the material in this book has been developed while I have been associated with the Foundation.

CBF is by no means a militant organization. It represents a broad spectrum of citizens, all of whom expect it to adhere to a regional view, to keep a balanced view, and to continue to work for the preservation of an environmentally healthy and aesthetically attractive Bay.

I believe the best of present-day conservationists are those who seek allies for the cause of an orderly management of resources, not those who exclude particular interests because they are easy targets. I often think of Pogo's prescient remark about the ever-elusive polluter: "We have met the enemy, and he is us."

The Chesapeake is fortunate in having top-flight scientists and professionals of every kind working on its behalf. You will gather from the following pages how much I rely on their contributions.

Finally, I am pleased to acknowledge the influence that *Man and Nature* and its author, George Perkins Marsh, have had on my thinking. First published in 1864, *Man and Nature; or Physical Geography As Modified by Human Action* is the record of the awakening of a cultivated mind to the basic truths of ecology. Marsh was a career diplomat, a lawyer. Stewart L. Udall explains his remarkable book and his reputation as the "fountainhead of the conservation movement" in these well-chosen words: "It was Marsh's omni-competence, his wholeness as a man, that made *Man and Nature* a bench mark. Within his mind there was an incessant dialogue between a naturalist, a humanist, a historian, a geographer, and a practical politician; it was this versatility which gave him dominion over a wide range of human knowledge."

If these pages mirror the slightest suspicion of the influence of such a dialogue, I'm delighted. I am quite convinced we serve ourselves and the Bay best when we consider it with an open mind and pursue its complexities with insatiable curiosity.

Arthur W. Sherwood

A distinctive characteristic of Bay charm—tranquility—is represented here:
moonlight illuminating the Eastern Shore at Kent Island, M.E. Warren

INTRODUCTION

Getting to know this extraordinary Bay is not easy. As informed an authority as Dr. Donald W. Pritchard, Director of the Chesapeake Bay Institute, delves deep this side of abracadabra to explain recent fishkills. Dr. William Hargis, Director of The Virginia Institute of Marine Sciences, recently warned conservation activists of what not to expect from the proposed Chesapeake Bay Hydraulic Model. (It will not, for instance, substitute for arduous biological fieldwork.) Moreover, while we properly look to scientists for fact and figure, we must not rely on their judgment as to what is our interest in the Bay, to what uses we wish it to be put, or in what ways conflicts of interests should be resolved.

The Need for a Sophisticated Personal Ecological Conscience

Inescapably, ultimate responsibility for the welfare of our Bay community rests squarely on the layman's shoulders—that is, with you and with me. It is a corollary of our independence from professional leadership. And it thrusts upon us the need to cultivate a sophisticated personal ecological conscience. "A thing is right," Aldo Leopold wrote in his *A Sand County Almanac,* "when it tends to preserve the integrity, stability and beauty of the biotic community. It is wrong when it tends otherwise." Perhaps no one has stated the basic tenet of an ecological conscience with more force and precision. If it speaks to us at all, it leaves us no choice but to understand our own biotic community—the Bay Country—well enough so we can tell, reasonably at best, intuitively if necessary, what in fact does preserve its integrity, stability and beauty and what does not. That takes knowing our environment from as many points of view as there are points of view to know.

Gibson Island at the mouth of the Magothy River is a good example of residential development which retains a maximum amount of open space and undisturbed shore. *The Baltimore Sun*

1. THE FINEST CRUISING GROUND IN THE WORLD

A Sailor's Point of View

Reed Creek, a short tributary of the Chester River north of Queenstown, is an idyllic remnant of unspoiled Chesapeake country.

Commercial clammers use the Creek as a convenient landing. A good haul can be 25 or 30 bushels of fat maninose from one boat, with enough "on top" or in an unfilled basket to make a meal for the browsing yachtsman.

Strong flood tides bring to the Creek a regular harvest of hungry crabs. Fifty to a hundred feet of trotline (about 20 chicken necks) will supply even the rawest amateur with all the hard-shellers he can handle.

Soft-shellers, a delectable reward for the patient stalker, are there too, and the Creek shores have fine grass bottoms for feeding sunfish and perch.

Because the Creek's narrow, twisting entrance between Tilghman Neck and Corsica Neck is nearly closed by Gordon Point, hidden in the apparent continuity of the Point's low-lying shoreline, sandy beach, and pine, it is infrequently visited. Its broad interior bay and long stretch of narrowing water are more often than not as empty of people, empty of boats, as the lost time when eagle and heron had it to themselves. This makes it, of course, an extraordinarily choice anchorage. The lone sailor, one who sneaks past Gordon Point as if escaping from prying eyes, does, in fact, virtually disappear from sight.

A few large farms take up most of the interior shore. Even these are only fleetingly seen. Thick hedges of honeysuckle rise from the water's edge. A perimeter of green—laurel and sumac, ivy, dogwood, oak, pine and poplar trees—encloses hundreds of acres of corn on one side and the creek on the other. Farm and field are as of another world.

Heron still dominate the Creek scene, both small and Great Blue. From dawn to dusk these prehistoric looking birds go squawking about their business. From shipboard, one sees them stalking prey along the shore or crisscrossing overhead, necks contracted, feet stretched far out behind. Better yet, from the silent, water-level view of a sailing dinghy, one drifts within 20 yards of feeding heron and becomes part of their

Reed Creek, a tributary of the Chester River. Diana Hardin Walker

wild world. To do so is to see every feather, to see the very gloss of their eyes, to watch hypnotized as with a dancer's precision and style they lift those long thin legs from the water, out and then down again, finally to stand immobile, a fashion of driftwood, ready to strike.

Great Blue Heron still dominate Reed Creek. The Baltimore *Sun*

Reed Creek is one example among thousands of what makes the Chesapeake the finest cruising ground in the world; one example among thousands of rivers, creeks, coves, and anchorages which make the Bay a recreational paradise.

Here, at Calvert Cliffs north of Cove Point, surveyors begin work on the Calvert Cliffs nuclear power plant. M.E. Warren

Robert and George Barrie cruised the Bay extensively at the turn of the century. Literate and observant, they give us in *Cruises, Mainly in the Bay of the Chesapeake,* a memorable account of one night in the mouth of the Piankatank River. "At sunset the scene was lovely: the Bay seemed like a tropical one, with white sand beaches surrounded with tall pines, each with a clump of branches at the top, sixty feet up; exactly like the palms in the East Indies. A glowing red sun and a pale pink and green sky completed the really tropical scene. That night we lounged on deck till after dark, and felt quite as though we had gone foreign: say to the South Sea Islands."

In this picture, the historic town of Oxford on the Tred Avon River is in the foreground. M.E. Warren

I know that feeling well. Going "foreign" is a commonplace occurrence for anyone venturing east to west or north to south within the confines of the Chesapeake and its tributaries. High banks and hardwoods characterize the upper western shores of the Bay. The Eastern Shore lies low to the water, hardly rising, for miles on end, beyond the reach of a flooding tide.

The Bay scene is "characterized neither by grandeur nor yet by quiet beauty alone." This combination of water, marsh, and woods is a typical Chesapeake blend. The Baltimore *Sun*

Intimacy characterizes rivers like the Wye, almost dike-like in the closeness of their banks and in the way they wind through rich, flat farmland; others, notably the Potomac, James, and York, are commercial waterways, grand and continental in their length, breadth, scope, and navigability. The Chester River is an authentic transplant from the British Isles.

There are many accounts of cruises on the Chesapeake. My favorite, a book I treasure, is *Vacation Cruising* by Dr. Joseph T. Rothrock, an eminent botanist and early conservationist. Published by J.B. Lippincott and Co. in 1884, now long since out of print, it gives us a true picture of the Bay as it was nearly a century ago.

Entering the Bay at its northern reaches, from the Chesapeake and Delaware Canal, Rothrock was overcome, as, thank goodness, a sailor is to this day, by the magnificence of the inland water as it opens to the South. "I never look from above the Bohemia River down toward the Bay," he wrote, "that this panorama does not impress me. It does so more and more the oftener I look at and enjoy it. To the south there is no visible limit. The bold, timber-covered bluffs east or west, with navigable rivers coming in between, run so that the horizon widens as one looks south. It is a scene characterized neither by grandeur nor yet by quiet beauty alone. The combination of water, of plains, and of hills in just the proper proportion is what completes this perfect picture; so perfect, too, that each season brings its own special beauty of the view. Back from the water a little distance, on higher ground, may be seen the comfortable houses of the farmers. Without indicating the presence of great wealth, the whole appearance of the region is one of thrift and abundance. There is no sign of the 'take-it-as-it-comes' spirit which is so common south of Annapolis; the air of the place rather speaks, 'Make the most of it.' Turkey Point, high and timber-clad, the location of an important light-house, stands like a sentinel between the Elk and the wide, shoal mouth of the Susquehanna River."

On his way south, Rothrock anchored for the night in Still Pond, on the Eastern Shore north of Chester River. Two notable characteristics of the Bay, then and now, were bound to make an impression on him—and did. He caught fish for dinner ("pike, yellow neds, perch, catfish"), fully appreciating the Bay's reputation as the seafood capital of the world, and he listened enthralled to the natural sounds of a Bay anchorage: "Every hour of day or night appeared to me to have brought some peculiar sound. In the morning we had catbirds, blackbirds, kingfishers, and fish-hawks; at noon, a family of crows, young and old, kept up a most persistent and vigorous cawing. Whether the last was a lesson in elocution for the junior members of the family I cannot say, though there appeared to be some object and some method in it. At night a legion of frogs gave us a prolonged high-toned serenade."

Inevitably, as Rothrock made his way down the Bay, the cumulative experience of river sailing and landlocked anchorages worked their magic on him.

Smith's Creek, at the mouth of the Potomac River: "The little bay, for such it was, in which we had anchored was completely landlocked, and not more than two hundred yards wide; yet it contained water enough for a good-sized vessel. This abundance of superior harbors may

River sailing and an abundance of superior harbors make the Bay the finest cruising ground in the world. Winter winds don't disturb these boats anchored in Spa Creek, Annapolis. M.E. Warren

be considered as a peculiarity in which the Chesapeake is pre-eminent.

"Milford Haven (Piankatank River) is still another of those surprises which constantly greet one yachting along the western shore of the Chesapeake. Now, as elsewhere, we were landlocked for the night. The entrance, which at first appeared too small to admit a vessel, widens out into a broad, deep mouth, and inside the harbor which it leads to a whole fleet of canoes and some good-sized schooners lay. During the evening spent there Mr. J. and Lew occupied themselves catching crabs. Half an hour of the sport was sufficient to cover the deck with vigorous pugnacious specimens, who the night through manifested their excessive vitality by threatening any one audacious enough to leave the cabin in the dark hours. However, this was more than compensated for when we came to enjoy them cooked. There is a difference in flavor of crabs, just as there is in that of oysters; and for both Milford Haven is justly famous. Cape May 'goodies,' served up with the oysters and crabs, make one even now, after the lapse of several months, remember our anchorage in the Piankatank with feelings of complete satisfaction."

Still Pond: "East and west the landlocked, beautiful pond spread out before us. Every one who is fond of the water has some ideal harbor which suggests perfect safety, easy landing on attractive shores, and what more each must add for himself to complete the picture. To me, when longing for a week on the water, this one, Still Pond, is ever uppermost in my mind. I often plan a whole vacation spent there.

"Our harbor in Antepoisen Creek (north of the Rappahannock) was another of the many beautiful ones, such as we had hitherto found. Near its head we were completely landlocked and had about two fathoms of water under the bow—just such a place as one can sleep most soundly in. There was no fear of anything."

Innumerable snug harbors and hundreds of miles of river sailing continue to this day to work their magic on Bay sailors. A lifetime of exploring them won't begin to exhaust the supply. I remember hearing the great Lowndes Johnson tell a youngster that he (Johnson) thought he "might have seen a little of the Bay." "How much?" the boy persisted. "Maybe a thousandth part," Johnson answered, and he meant it. Lowndes Johnson lived his long life on the Bay; sailed it every year till he was past 80. He designed the Comet and gave away the plans so more kids could have one. His mild manners, gentleness, and kindness are remembered and well represent the character of the country to which he gave so much.

For those who would enjoy the Bay today, I cannot too vigorously emphasize that the changes to the Chesapeake since Rothrock sailed it are relatively superficial. The Grandiflora Magnolias and Mimosas along the banks of the James River still mingle their perfume with wild honeysuckle and rose. It is still possible to sail with a school of porpoise at your bow, not lost in ocean distances, but hours away from a safe

Chapel Point, St. Ignatius Church, overlooking the Potomac River. M.E. Warren

harbor and never long out of sight of a friendly shore. The Bald Eagle is now a rare and endangered species, but careful looking is still rewarding and Osprey seem to be more plentiful than they were a few years ago. It is still possible to leave a harried city life—Washington or Baltimore— and be on the Bay within an hour, underway an hour later, and into a

The Chesapeake is ideal habitat for the Osprey, and many may still be seen on the Bay. This pair is nesting on a duck blind near Hambleton Island, Broad Creek. Frank Davis

river at anchor before dark, miraculously transported to a stillness, a naturalness, a peacefulness that seems impossibly close to the movement and noises one has left behind. The "dreaded" Bay squall is as much an adventure now as it was for John Smith, and so, on quite another plane, is star gazing on a summer's night. I often wonder what

The first signs of a Chesapeake squall are evident and unmistakable. Seen from the air above Rhode River, a solid wall of black (background) appears as ominous as it does from the water. M.E. Warren

makes such a night on the Bay so totally satisfying. Perhaps Rothrock has the answer: "I have companions who have sought wisdom in the books until they are pale, and who have lost the elastic step one should have until his head is silvered. They can name each star and tell its distance from the earth in miles, but they have never laid down and gone to sleep while looking up at them, and wondering, not studying, how big those stars were. I think these persons have missed an element of education which would send them back to work wiser and better and healthier for their gazing."

Cruising the Chesapeake, I hasten to advise the uninitiated, is not all perfume and roses. Consider, for instance, this day on the Bay.

You arise early, sniff the fresh morning air, take a dip, rouse your tardy crew, demand (and get) a hearty breakfast, pass judgment on the day as perfect for a passage south, and set sail. All's well, or so it seems. By mid-morning your early breeze is no longer nicely moderate or even acceptably light—it has "dropped," as the saying goes, and you find yourself becalmed.

A totally flat Bay calm in the middle of July or August or September can make you wonder quickly why you didn't stay home. Swimming may relieve the torture, but not for long. An awning provides the same breathless shade you find below. Your auxiliary motor, of course, is on the blink. So you sit. Conversation lags. Life becomes wearisome and dreary. Worse is yet to come.

No breeze has yet stirred to relieve the enervating heat. The sun continues its relentless bake. You are aggravated, irritated, frustrated— and now suddenly alarmed. For the first signs of a Chesapeake squall are evident, and unmistakable: clouds, a darkening sky, flashes of lightning, and absolute, impermeable stillness; the quiet before the storm.

What soon breaks upon you with apparent vindictiveness is wind which gusts to 50 knots, rain too fierce to face, and a chaotic sea. Fortunately, you're prepared. You've shortened sail to a reefed main. You've checked your course, taken bearings on visible shores and lights, figured where to run for maximum sea room, what lee shore to avoid. Then the fun begins. You're never dead sure where you're going or where you are. You keep the presence of that lee shore uppermost in mind. You decide you should change course. You try to come about. Wind and wave work against you—you fail. You fall off, get headway and try again. Again those damnable choppy seas and shrieking head-winds work against you. Your shortened rig just won't bring you round. You panic. Not visibly. Not so you loose your hand on the tiller. But enough to experience one moment of fear. You think you may be beaten. If seems as if the gods have chosen to be perverse and have perversely chosen you for sport.

The Chester River winds in an undulating series of graceful curves to the charming houses of Chestertown. M.E. Warren

In the end you bring her round. You get in after dark tired, hungry, wet and immensely happy. Tomorrow, you know, will be a lay day, a long, slow dawdling day in the sun, in a snug harbor with nothing to do but loaf and catch crabs and watch the women work.

And the day after that you'll be up early sniffing the morning breeze again, anxious to get underway. Where you go in this world of a thousand choices will depend partly on the weather and a lot on your previous experience cruising the Bay. Because soon enough you will have your own favorite haunts. For world-renowned sailor and racer Carleton Mitchell, it's the Wye River, "in its own way worthy of comparison with the Aegean, the Baltic, the Caribbean, the Pacific—a rambling few miles of solitude which seep into the soul, quiet green lanes of peace after the boisterous blue wastes of ocean Finisterre and I had known together."

For me, it's the Chester River on a fall cruise. Ducks, geese and swan; the browns, reds, oranges, and scarlets of oak, gum, poplar, elm, sassafras, and beech; a lovelier farm than the one just passed around the next bend in an increasingly intimate river which winds in an undulating series of graceful curves for 25 miles, from its meeting with the Bay at Love Point-Swan Point to the charming houses of Chestertown. Is such an experience memorable? Will it last you through the roughest winter? Will it convince you that the Bay is, in fact, the finest cruising ground in the world? With towering restraint I answer all in a word—*yes.*

The nuclear power plant shown here at Calvert Cliffs is one of a dozen planned to serve the power needs of a region which grew from 11 million to 15 million people in ten years. Baltimore Gas & Electric Co.

II. CHAOS OR A NEW MANAGEMENT OF RESOURCES

A Consumer's Point of View

Points of view well worth listening to were expressed by many of those who participated in the 1971 Citizens Program Conference, none with more pith than the consumer's viewpoint given by Dr. Aiton, Conference Chairman. Edward W. Aiton, agriculturist, conservationist, educator—pre-eminently a Bay Country gentleman—opened the Conference with accustomed balance: "This is not doomsday!" he said. "We are not proposing to push the panic button and send all hands to their legislature on Monday morning with petitions to stop all man-made developments so that we can return to the good life of Henry Thoreau. But today is not Utopia either. We are moving toward dooms-day and away from Utopia at an alarming rate."

Ambivalence, as Aiton admits, is the often confusing and worrisome lot of today's Bay consumer. Seduced on one hand by pleasures and conveniences, from new bridges (the second Chesapeake Bay Bridge at Sandy Point), new power plants (the nuclear plant at Calvert Cliffs is one of a dozen planned), and new residential developments (proposed, at this instant, for Wye and Goodwin Islands, Bennett Point, South River), he is numbed on the other hand by stark statistics of regional growth: 11 million population in 1960; 15 million in 1970; the prospect of 30 million within the next 50 years! What that suggests, in the words of Robert T. Dennis, formerly director of the Central Atlantic Environment Service, is "Chaos—uncontrolled growth, community sprawl, industrial locations determined by economic factors more than anything else, creeping pollution, declining quality of life for all of us."

Alternatives for Bay Consumers

Alternatives for Bay consumers are easily recognized. One course is to cry loudly and do nothing; admit helplessness and stoke the fires of despair. Another is to join in serious efforts to reorder management of Bay resources. A reordering, if successful, will treat the Chesapeake as the integrated ecosystem (environmental niche to which specific species adapt) it is, not as one part Virginia and one part Maryland, one part Talbot County, one part Queen Anne's County.

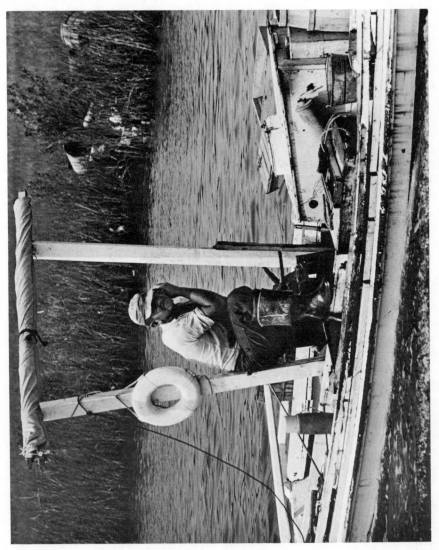

This Smith Island crabber is characteristic of the independent Bay waterman. M.E. Warren

III. GOOD NEWS ABOUT MODERN TECHNOLOGY

An Economic Point of View

Garrett Hardin, author of *Nature and Man's Fate, Science Conflict and Society* and other books relating to the environment, is perhaps best known for a single phrase: "the tragedy of the commons." Its application to the economics of Bay Country life is striking.

The "tragedy" of the phrase refers to the irreparable damage that results from harvesting crops without concern for their future, notably from common ground for which the farmer, herdsman or waterman has no personal responsibility. It is the tragedy, in words best appreciated around the Chesapeake, of a diminishing supply of oysters, clams, fish and crab, because those who harvest them have little if any responsibility for their production; feel free—in fact obliged—to take all they can get. Unlike private ownership of the source of production, a commons invites exploitation by all those who are competing for its benefits.

A statement of the problem of commons ownership suggests the solution: abolish the commons and substitute an acceptable form of leasehold to qualified tenants. Unfortunately, when economic considerations are counted, simple solutions become complicated and obvious ones disappear.

Watermen operating in a commons context can get by with minimum overhead (one boat) and a crew often drawn from a single family (father and sons). Take away the commons, and this characteristic, lovable, stubborn old salt of the Bay Country disappears into corporate enterprises sufficiently capitalized to undertake private mariculture. Nor is the waterman a lonely example of developing problems when realities associated with the economics of production are considered.

Chesapeake Trouble Spots

A recent list of locations on the Bay hardest hit by some form of "trouble" (sewage and eutrophication, oil spillage, waste and resource consumption by heavy industry, sediment, chemical killers (pesticides, etc.), litter, light industry, dredging spoil, engineering works, fossil power, and nuclear power—ranked, in that order, by Dr. Pritchard) names the following 14 areas:

(1) Chesapeake and Delaware Canal (modification of freshwater flow, dredging and spoil disposal, shipping, oil spills)

(2) Susquehanna River (nutrients, modification of freshwater flow, sediments, energy, fisheries)

(3) Back River (municipal waste, nutrients)

(4) Patuxent River (thermal addition, nutrients)

(5) Calvert Cliffs (thermal addition, radionuclides, political problems)

(6) Cove Point (proposed liquid natural gas terminal, dredging, spoil disposal)

(7) Rappahannock River (freshwater flow modification, industrial wastes, area of relatively low stress, nutrients)

(8) Upper York River (industrial wastes, freshwater flow modification, wetlands, fisheries)

(9) Lower York River (thermal addition, oil transport, dredging, spoil disposal, wetland alteration, fisheries, residential wastes)

(10) Upper Tidal James River (above Jamestown) (industrial and municipal wastes, dredging, heavy metals, human health (bacterial counts)

(11) Lower Tidal James River (below Jamestown) (industrial and municipal wastes, transportation (water and vehicular), spoil disposal, dredging, thermal addition, fisheries, heavy metals)

(12) Hampton Roads (transportation (water and vehicular), ship waste, spoil disposal, recreation)

(13) Nansemond, Elizabeth and Lafayette Rivers (heavy metals, municipal wastes, fisheries, urbanization, oil handling and transport, shipping, shoreline modifications)

(14) Lower Eastern Shore (economy, agricultural wastes, wetlands, fisheries, erosion, access to water, industrial development)

The list was prepared by the Research Planning Committee of the Chesapeake Research Consortium (C.R.C.) financed by the National Science Foundation, as an unprecedented joining of the principal research institutions associated with the Bay—The Johns Hopkins University (Chesapeake Bay Institute), University of Maryland (Natural Resources Institute and Chesapeake Bay Laboratories), Virginia Institute of Marine Science, and the Smithsonian Institution.

A Harsh Indicator of Hard Choices

This list of trouble spots serves well as a harsh indicator of the hard choices, largely economic choices, implicit in every environmental problem. Take, for instance, the proposed deepening and widening of the Chesapeake and Delaware Canal. Environmentalists are understandably concerned about the possibility that a deepened and widened canal will deflect Susquehanna freshwater from the upper Bay to the

The Chesapeake and Delaware Canal is one of the 14 locations hardest hit by some form of trouble currently affecting the resources of the Bay. M.E. Warren

If technological innovations, like the replacing of these skipjacks with powerboats for oyster dredging, invariably produce increased pollution of the environment, the future for the Bay is bleak. M.E. Warren

Delaware Bay, thus substantially affecting the salinity content of both areas. Commercial interests, especially those associated with trade and industry in and around the international port of Baltimore, insist that a deeper canal is essential if the port is to accommodate the deeper draft ships presently engaged in world trade. The public seems caught in the middle: approve environmental degradation and encourage trade or protect the environment and throttle trade. Cost vs. benefits.

Stark pessimism often follows a discussion of the economics of a healthy environment, and the reasons are apparent. If "externalities" (production costs borne by the public, like air pollution in the manufacture of soap) cannot be prohibited without wiping out profits, pessimism is justified. As ecologist Barry Commoner exhaustively documents (*The Closing Circle*), if technological innovations (like synthetic fibers for cotton) invariably produce increased pollution of the environment, pessimism is justified. If externalities and technologically polluting innovations are essential ingredients of profitable production, pessimism is justified. But are they? Some think not. A far more realistic view, in my opinion, holds that environmentally conscious technology can eliminate externalities without crippling production or undermining reasonable profits.

Environmentally Conscious Technology

The rationale for this freshening approach comes, surprisingly, from the very statistics which document the impact of technologically damaging production.

Data collected on the characteristics of our production of goods and services for the 25-year postwar period 1946 to 1971 indicate an increase in levels of pollution far in excess of either population increase (42%) or the increase in spending per person (50% in terms of GNP per capita). Examples given by Commoner include: nitrogen oxides from automobiles, up 630%; tetraethyl lead from gasoline, up 415%; mercury from chloralkali plants, up 2,100%; synthetic pesticides, up 270%; inorganic nitrogen fertilizer, up 789%; non-returnable beer bottles, up 595%. Commoner understandably concludes that the real villain of the piece is environmentally damaging technological innovation. But Commoner overlooks, in my opinion, the all-important fact that the years he considered are as notable for their existence prior to environmental awareness as they are for their devastatingly poor environmental track record. I would appreciate it if anyone reading this, particularly those contributing to our GNP during the postwar years, would give careful, objective thought to the extent to which he (or she) was conscious of environmental deterioration during this period. For my part, till about 1960, I am certain I could not have given a middling definition of ecology. I well remember a conversation I had during this time with a distinguished engineer. I learned that exhaust from buses and autos was an "inconsequential" factor in the quality of urban air.

Implicit, then, in Commoner's statistics is a reasonable basis for assuming that technological innovation in the years ahead, during a period when the environment is much in the picture, will produce gains as significant for their impact on environmental protection as it did heretofore in environmental pollution. One specific example within my personal experience will not prove the point, but it is revealing. I hope others are able to contribute their own hard evidence of what is happening to Bay resources now that modern technology is ecologically motivated.

The manned, electronically sophisticated Coast Guard station at Thomas Point Light is a striking example of technology working for a safe, healthy environment.
M.E. Warren

An Example of Modern Technology Ecologically Motivated

Power lines have been around for a long time and for a long time have given the impression that the convenience of an electric light had to be paid for in cross-country acres scarred by bulldozers, stripped of trees, and subject to serious erosion. I had such a picture in mind when I went out recently to inspect for myself the nearly completed line which begins at Calvert Cliffs and terminates 50 miles inland at the Waugh Chapel Station of the Baltimore Gas and Electric Company.

I shall be careful in reporting what I found; it all seems so good. First the road, that inevitable "service" way that used to stretch in an unending straight line, leveling hills, banishing trees, and looking like business—nothing but. There is a road, but it looks to me as if Frederick Law Olmstead had a hand in laying it out. In a word, it is landscaped. It goes up and down hills, around gulleys, between mature stands of trees on a curvilinear path ideally suited for cross-country hiking. If there is a single mile of it entirely planned for utilitarian use, I did not see it. Rather it invites comparison to a country road designed to show off its surroundings.

What next caught my attention was the individualized treatment of each supporting tower. I am not an engineer. I am not a landscape architect. But I have seen enough power lines to expect large expanses of concrete and substantial digging and filling to accommodate the tremendous weight of towers on irregular ground. Here I found no concrete except for footings. Apparently crushed stone has been substituted for concrete and exposed areas have been seeded. Gabions and jute netting have been used extensively, with the result that disturbed areas already appear stabilized. To the extent to which I can judge, each tower is designed for its particular location, and every area subject to erosion has been protected.

Overall, I got the distinct impression that sediment loss will not occur, that erosion has been controlled, that selective attention has been given to saving trees and preserving ground cover, that storm water will not wash out from culverts provided for it, and that the configuration of the land has been respected—aesthetically and practically. I have no idea what this "treatment" cost. I know the money was environmentally well spent.

This is one example of technology working for a healthy environment. Do you know of others? Is evidence accumulating to substantiate economic optimism? Are we enough into an era of ecological sophistication to begin to see a new pattern of statistics emerge?

A section of a power line from Calvert Cliffs to Waugh Chapel Station. An
example of modern technology working for the environment, each tower is
designed for its particularized location, and every area subject to erosion has
been protected. Baltimore Gas & Electric Co.

IV. ENLIGHTENED COMMERCIALISM

A Businessman's Point of View

W. Gregory Halpin, deputy director of the Maryland Port Authority, is author of more important facts about the business of the Port of Baltimore than anyone else—friend or foe. For instance:

The Port, the principal maritime industry of the Bay, "has a total impact on the economy of the State of Maryland in excess of 1.5 billion each year"—15% of the gross State product.

150,000 people in Maryland (1/5 of the total work force) are employed at jobs related to Port activities.

$40,000,000 of taxes per year are generated from Port operations.

An average 10,000 tons of general cargo are handled by Port facilities every day.

Baltimore enjoys two major passageways connecting it to the Atlantic: 150 miles via Cape Henry and Cape Charles, 125 miles via the Chesapeake and Delaware Canal.

In excess of 10,000 ships carrying more than 40,000,000 tons of freight per year use Baltimore.

The Port is "Maryland's greatest commercial asset."

Translating facts like these into a coherent statement of the Bay's proper function generates as much sweat on the businessman's brow as it does for the most scientifically oriented environmentalist. Both must face up to the mind-crunching task of assigning priorities for the use of resources no longer considered limitless or expendable by anyone.

The Magic of Creative Compromise

Not surprisingly, the vocabulary of the Halpin approach offers no trace of phrases like zero population growth, economic stagnation, or moratorium on shoreline use for industrial purposes (à la Delaware Bay), words bristling with conservationist militarism and positively anathema to every blend of commercial interest. What does characterize Greg Halpin's position is what might be designated enlightened commercialism. He is on the one hand traditionally progressive and competi-

The Port of Baltimore, Maryland's greatest commercial asset. M.E. Warren

tive: "Maritime commerce is a keystone to the stable economy of the State; therefore, the State in its own self-interest must do everything possible to protect, nourish and expand this industry." He is also environmentally conscious: "We can have cargo and crabs. We can have oilers and oysters." He is sensitive to the magic of creative compromise: the resources of the Bay can be progressively developed "without conflict or damage to any particular segment. . .only if there is recognition that there be a place for and room for development of each of these segments and resources."

While this is a difficult point to judge, it is possible the businessman is more often misrepresented by conservationists than vice versa! The emotional impact of a plea for "no more dams" (David Brower) stands a good chance of overpowering the merits of a technical argument. In my opinion, this is all the more reason why those of us aspiring to environmental reasonableness must often take another look.

To Dredge or Not to Dredge

An excellent case in point involves a controversy close to the vital interests of the Port of Baltimore: to dredge or not to dredge a deeper channel. The problem is one of what to do with tons of spoil, material probably toxic and always, at best, an offensive ooze.

At first glance, it would appear that the dredging proposal is another instance of environmental rape. Why must the Bay accommodate larger and deeper draft ships necessitating the possible diversion of fresh water from the Susquehanna, and inevitably producing tons of spoil? Must the Port "progress" at the expense of an increasingly imposed-upon natural resource? What is wrong with a Port which presently produces an annual income in excess of $1,000,000,000?

A second glance answers some, but not all, of these questions. The Port of Baltimore is in a highly competitive position—with Great Lakes ports served by the Saint Lawrence Seaway, with New York, Boston, New Orleans, and Norfolk-Hampton Roads. To meet the competition, it must stay up-to-date, and in these days that means being fully willing and able to handle containerization. This new form of transporting cargo has revolutionized the transportation industry, and Baltimore as a harbor is a dead duck unless it can attract the larger, deeper draft container ships. In this instance, then, "progress" is a matter of dire necessity, not in any sense growth for growth's sake. As Greg Halpin puts it, "The Bay must remain the passageway to the Port, and the Port must have freedom for expansion to meet competitive threats. Those threats are very real. Having survived such dangers as the Saint Lawrence Seaway, facility obsolescence and the loss of favorable inland rate differentials, the Port and, therefore, the State now faces the threats proposed by. . .containerization."

Maritime commerce is a keystone to the stable economy of the Bay Country. The "old" Bay Bridge—a single span—is shown here. The bridge is now a double span, dramatic evidence of regional growth and the problems attending to it. M.E. Warren

Still another look takes us to the point at which, it seems, some vital interests of someone must suffer. Surprisingly, in this instance, not so! While the question of fresh water diversion is still unresolved, there is substantial agreement that spoil material contained within dikes around the eroding shores of Hart and Miller Islands (offshore near the entrance to the Port) will not only protect the Bay from toxic material, but will also eventually produce valuable new bayside property suitable for recreational purposes.

The Partition Principle—Cluster Development

Not every conservation-industry confrontation has such a happy ending. Not every businessman has enough breadth of vision to combine highly refined acquisitive instincts with a gut feeling for the precariousness of natural resources. And certainly not every environment has a community of scientific institutions ingenious enough to work out acceptable solutions to problems like spoil disposal. From a businessman's point of view, however, the Bay Country is eminently partitionable. It has already demonstrated that if commercial interests are clustered in commercial locations like Baltimore and Norfolk, the broad reaches between will not be punished—"all the resources of the Bay can be developed to their full potential cooperatively and without the infringement of the one upon the other."

It is precisely this reasoning which makes the proposed liquid natural gas pier at Cove Point appear to be so grievously, avoidably wrong.

Bridge crossing the C & D Canal at Chesapeake City. The Canal is a vital link between the Atlantic and Bay ports. Dept. of Economic Development

V. UNITY AND CHANGE

A Geological Point of View

So far we have looked at the Bay from nonscientific points of view. Enter now the professors, the first of whom is Dr. Markley Gordon Wolman at Johns Hopkins University. He is a geologist and geographer. He "reads" the Bay in terms of its ecological unity and dynamic character, emphasizing the interdependence of its various parts and the way they change, subject as they all are to the persistent forces of wind, tide, and man.

Dr. Wolman's Bay statistics are remarkable in themselves. It comes as no little surprise to me that the total drainage area of the Bay is 64,000 square miles, approximately the size of the State of Washington! No less of a surprise is the fact that this 195-mile-long Bay, with 150 rivers, creeks, and branches, its 4,600 miles of tidewater shoreline, and 4,300 square miles of surface water has a mean depth of only 21 feet! The Bay is a "shallow pan" indeed, all the more susceptible because of it to the rate of erosion and sedimentation which are the most visible features of the Bay's "dynamic character."

Nothing puzzles the layman like myself more than the realization that this visible change—erosion which gobbled up the whole of Sharps Island, all 450 acres of it, since the middle of the 19th century; sedimentation which currently flows into Bay waters at the startling rate of some eight million tons per year; a constant shifting of bars (sailors beware), changing shoreline, and shifting channels (sailors excuse)—that all this shifting, moving, wearing, is in large part the inevitable result of natural forces. That we cannot really put the blame on man for the disappearance of Sharps Island. That our "geologic history is imminent." That the Bay is a relatively "new" and "young" environment, not more than eight to ten thousand years old, the result of the last glacial melting which flooded the Susquehanna River Valley. That we are changing because we are still "shaking down" as a young ecosystem. In Dr. Wolman's words, "The so-called 'natural' scene is, in this region, neither static nor even ponderous in its rate of movement." This puzzles a layman like myself, because I would feel more comfortable, more sure of myself as a conservationist, if I didn't have to think of apparently deleterious change to the Bay Country as possibly in the very nature of things, ordered not by man, but by the rains and winds and currents. The complexity of an ecosystem like the Bay makes life tough for all of us.

Regional Planning and Zoning

The point of view of a geologist and geographer has noteworthy significance for those of us who are interested in regional planning and zoning for the Bay Country. Should not the social apparatus of an ecosystem match its natural subject? If what happens to the quality of water in Onancock Creek affects the life of a blue crab breeding in the shoals of Eastern Bay, can we govern either place with good sense without governing them together? If 64,000 square miles draining to the Bay is sensitive throughout to what happens to any of its parts, can

Sedimentation is one of the most visible features of the Bay's dynamic character. Constant dredging is required to keep channels navigable. M.E. Warren

we partition off any portion of it for the purpose of "planning" its use and development? If the Bay region is still perceptibly settling its geologic destiny, who but the most intrepid planner—exceedingly so—would set out to plan for the use and development of the Bay country of Virginia alone. If the Bay region is so susceptible to change, a process clearly exacerbated by man, should we leave it planless, a patchwork of wildlife management laws and uncoordinated zoning? Many of those I talk to these days around the Bay think the Bay Country needs regional planning and zoning. I agree.

The Bay, looking north towards Cove Point, a few square miles among 64,000 comprising an ecologically unified drainage area. M.E. Warren

The Susquehanna River alone produces a mean discharge of 40,000 cubic feet per second of fresh water into the Bay. Here one small section near Havre de Grace provides sport for fishermen. M.E. Warren

VI. THE MYSTERIOUS FORCES OF AN ESTUARY

An Oceanographic Point of View

For me, the point of view of an oceanographer like Dr. Donald William Pritchard, director of the Chesapeake Bay Institute, is perhaps the most exotic of any of the many approaches to an understanding of the wonderful ways of this estuary. An oceanographer thinks in terms of such mysterious forces as tides, currents, salinity, and photosynthesis.

I imagine an oceanographer thinking of the Bay as a giant lung, its 4,300 square miles of surface water as sensitive as the capillaries which aerate our blood. The Bay "breathes," taking in and giving out dissolved oxygen as regularly as we inhale and exhale. Dissolved oxygen is added to the water through exchange at the air-water interface and through photosynthesis; it is lost through plant decay, and through the breathing processes of its animal life. It is, therefore, extraordinarily subject to abuse and difficult to diagnose. Why does the Bay suffer "fish kills" about as regularly as many of us catch colds? If I am not mistaken, not as much is known about fish kills as is known about the common cold—and the future of both is doubtful only as to when, not whether, we will be affected by them again. Irritating? Frustrating? Infuriating? Yes, but less so when we are not simplistic in our understanding of the Bay; when we think of it as a fragile resource influenced as much by the behavior of the weather as by the misbehavior of man.

An Estuary

An estuary is a coastal body of water open to the sea within which sea water is measurably diluted by fresh water drainage from the land. The Bay is a "partially mixed estuary." In Dr. Pritchard's words, "This is because the salinity distribution, while showing an increase with depth, indicating the estuary is not completely mixed vertically, does not show a sharp boundary separating an upper, low salinity layer from an intruding wedge-shaped bottom layer of high salinity, which is characteristic of a class of estuaries having small tidal currents, and which are called salt wedge estuaries." What this signifies to a layman like myself is that we are gloriously fortunate in having an estuary which is fed daily from the nutrient sources of over 150 fresh water tributaries by land, and by sea from the Atlantic, via the wide inviting capes of Charles and Henry. The Susquehanna alone produces a mean discharge of 40,000 cubic feet per second of fresh water into the Bay. Tidal currents, and the less appreciated net nontidal circulation of water (a vertical pattern which empties the Bay from the surface layers while replenishing it at the bottom) operate like a giant flushing device. The result is that the Bay is regularly cleaned up, cleared out, and refreshed. Had Lake Erie been as lucky, it would not now be irreparably damaged. Had the Bay formed its principal hydraulic features with less advantage, we would not have the time we presently enjoy to "save" it. As it is, we have only so much time—how much no one really knows—to see to it that our advantages are not wasted.

The most easily remembered and most significant two numbers associated with the Bay are 0 and 30: 0—30 ppt. (parts per thousand), representing the Bay's range of salinity, and 0—30° C. (degrees centigrade), representing its range of temperature. In an estuarine system like the Bay, what lives and what does not depends largely on the variation in the temperature of the water and on the distribution and circulation of its saline content.

Superstorm "Agnes" (spring 1972) dramatically proved the point. The Bay region was flooded. Abnormal amounts of fresh water and sediment poured into it. Soft shell clam bottoms were critically injured. Oyster bars were silted over. The sea nettle vanished in parts of the upper Bay. One man's loss (commercial clammers) was another's gain (swimmers), but both needed no scientific equipment to qualify them as expert witnesses on the effects of the storm.

Fortunately, salinity and temperature can be measured and fully appreciated without the help of an "Agnes." Try it. Develop your own set of norms for a particular favorite spot on the Bay. You will be surprised to find how revealing it is to compare one month's reading with another; to draw your own conclusions about the current condition of that part of the Bay you care about most. How to go about it and the simple equipment you need for the job are described in the CBF Ecology Cruise Guide. (See Appendix.)

VII. THE CROWN JEWEL OF ESTUARIES

A Biological Point of View

"The Chesapeake Bay is the crown jewel of the 850 estuaries and bays along the several coasts of the United States. It is the largest bay in the country, more valuable for human uses than any other estuary, and vulnerable to destruction from human use and abuse." Dr. L. Eugene Cronin, director of the Natural Resources Institute of the University of Maryland, author of this statement, represents a point of view at least passingly familiar to all of us. Dr. Cronin is a marine biologist. A marine biologist thinks of the Bay in terms of its "biota," the flora and fauna which inhabit it, including, but by no means restricted to the following: our Chincoteague oyster (transplanted from the Bay to Chincoteague Sound for last-minute flavoring); our blue crab (enjoyed best hard, soft, flaked or caked, indisputably the finest eating crab in the world); our long-neck, soft-shell clam (preferably steamed, dipped in butter, and enjoyed as a main course; and delicious as a chowder, as they are often served in New England); our Susquehanna shad (indisputably the finest eating fish in the world, especially when baked with its roe and served with a light, well-chilled wine); our terrapin (once everyday food for slaves, now get it if you can and don't forget the beaten biscuits); and our waterfowl in season—not for sale. Along with the 250 varieties of fish which use the Bay and species of plants and animals as inedible but ecologically significant as the nudibranch (the "naked shrimp" which likes to eat sea nettle polyps), these are the focus of attention of the marine biologist. What comes as a surprise to me is that this point of view concerns itself with the vulnerability of the relatively short food chain which characterizes the Bay ecosystem.

You will remember that from a geologist's point of view the Chesapeake estuarine system is young, only 8 to 10 thousand years old. The living organisms of the area, therefore, have had to make major adaptations to a strange environment in a relatively short period of time. A shallow pan of mixed salt and fresh water is biologically a rather rare environment, one to which many organisms from exclusively fresh or salt water or deeper water cannot adapt. Those that do may well prove to be as prolific as our crab and clam, but they are nonetheless one of a few species more dependent on one another than if they had a larger

The clams, crabs, oysters, and fish shown here all came from the Bay's teeming waters. All are easy to cook; all are delicious. M.E. Warren

The harbor at Crisfield, seafood capital of the Bay. Bay delicacies are part of a relatively short and vulnerable food chain. M.E. Warren

A salt marsh on Smith Island. Marshes, submerged aquatic plants, and phytoplankton are the producers of food for Bay animals. M.E. Warren

choice of natives to dine on. That explains their vulnerability. Damage to one species among many (a "long" food chain) is more easily absorbed by the native biota than damage to any one of a few: a limited food supply is more susceptible to loss than an abundant one. So the plants and animals of the Bay live a precarious existence, a fact of consequence to those of us at the end of the line who can do most to minimize dangers and manage a healthy environment.

Bay Inventory

An inventory of the Bay's biota was briefly summarized by Dr. Cronin at the Wye Institute's Governor's Conference on the Bay. His summary is a useful tool for the observer of the Bay scene. The next time you are out on the water or on its shores look for:

(1) The Producers (plants)
    (a) Marshes
    (b) Submerged aquatics
    (c) Phytoplankton (microscopic drifting plants)
(2) The Consumers (animals)
    (a) Bottom, including the crab, oyster, and clam
    (b) Drifters, including the larval stage of most of the Bay animals—zooplankton
    (c) Swimmers
        Resident fish, like perch, anchovy, and rock
        Spawners, like shad and herring
        Visitors, like blues, flounder, and cobia
    (d) Birds, mammals, and reptiles

For the purposes of observing the biota of the Bay intelligently, I find it helpful to rely on this very simple scheme. Are we looking at consumers or producers? Both are part of a relatively short, and therefore vulnerable, estuarine food chain. But we should not make the mistake of assuming that a "short" food chain is an easy one to understand—in depth. The trained Bay biologist is aware of more than 2,600 species of organisms indigenous to the system. The possible interactions of these species are estimated, by Drs. Andrew McErlean and Catherine Kerby, to number in the trillions. A little imagination translates these pyramiding numbers into an important fact-of-life conclusion. Every day we humans are putting in or taking out of the Bay in ways that directly affect its biota and in ways that may well modify the very structure and dynamics—the equilibrium and health—of the system as a whole.

In Volume 13, Supplement, of *Chesapeake Science,* a quarterly published by The Natural Resources Institute of the University of

Every day we humans are putting in or taking out of the Bay in ways that directly affect its biota. Here is a variety of filth in Annapolis harbor. M.E. Warren

Maryland, Drs. McErlean and Kerby give the following clear example of the possible sequence of events from human activity on the Bay (construction and operation of a power plant) to its biological effect.

Human Activity
Construction and Operation of a Power Plant

Environmental Modification
Modification of a River Flow
Diversion of Water to condenser surfaces

Primary Environmental Effect
Modification of Salinity Pattern

At a Maryland power plant, intake and outfall are about two miles apart. Salinity gradients in this section of the river are steep, and salinity differential (intake-outfall comparison) can amount to several ppt. (parts per thousand).

Biological Effect
Plankton Community Affected

Higher salinity water, with entrained plants and animals, undergoes inversion; some probable effects:

(1) phytoplankton community removed from "nutritional" source, i.e., turbidity impairs light penetration—less phytoplankton respiration.
(2) zooplankton subjected to salinity shock.

The preceding example should not be read as "proving" more than that specific human activity produces an observable impact on the biota of the Bay. Left glaringly unproven is whether production of power is worth the impact it has on the natural state of the Bay. Put another way, the example alerts us to the fact that the Bay is brimfull of plants and animals which cannot be sucked into a foreign environment without, alas, expiring on the way through. It alerts us to the fact that power may well require from the teeming waters of the Bay an identifiable and controlled loss of life. Not to recognize this fact and deal with it honestly is treacherously tempting. Yet neither nostalgia for the vanished days of tepee living nor a predatory blindness to the inevitable biological impact of industry is an acceptable biological alternative.

An abandoned car in a tributary of the Rappahannock. M.E. Warren

VIII. IMITATING THE EXPERTS

A Learner's Point of View

Knowing more about the biota of the Bay than a few common names and being able to identify species among the estimated 1,162 plants and 1,488 animals indigenous to it is a game more of us should play. The rewards are good eating, venturesome foraging, the inevitable kick one gets from an outdoors experience, and a better understanding of the whole Bay system.

Recently I spent a long weekend with Euell Gibbons on the Piankatank River. The time was early spring; the occasion a Chesapeake Bay Foundation field trip organized by CBF trustees John Page Williams and Russell Scott.

Euell Gibbons, author of the famous stalking series, including *Stalking the Blue-Eyed Scallop* and *Stalking the Wild Asparagus,* as a boy tracking alone the vastness of our southwest, began early to develop a talent, one might even say a genius, for survival in the wilderness. Years of foraging from mountaintop and seashore have made him an authority. Edible plants and animals, their identification, harvesting and preparation comprise a world he has explored and exploited for the benefit of millions. His followers are rarely those who wish to survive in the wilderness; they are those who wish wild places and wild things to survive in them.

I was not surprised to find that Gibbons appreciates the Bay. Shortly after our time together on the Piankatank, he wrote in *Organic Gardening* (August 1972): "I live more than a hundred miles from the nearest approach of Chesapeake Bay, but several times a year I find myself drawn in that direction for boating, fishing, foraging or just plain beachcombing. I love this great inland sea and its miles of shoreline. If this bay is ruined for recreational use, the quality of my life will be diminished. Fortunately, the Bay is far from dead, and although abused and injured in many places, with loving care it can completely recover. It still produces thousands of tons of fish, crabs, oysters, and clams. Sport fishermen still throng its waters and few come back empty-handed. You can find hundreds of miles of uninhabited shorelines and pristine tidal creeks to anchor a boat in primeval solitude or camp in lonely splendor."

What we found together that spring weekend on the Piankatank should inspire everyone with a taste for adventure to get out onto the shores of the Bay. Gibbons' account sparkles with his characteristic vigor and intelligence.

Euell Gibbons, master forager, is shown here after a venturesome day in the field. Daniel Kramer

"We spent the evening at the Fishing Bay Yacht Club, discussing our plans and studying color slides of the edible plants we expected to find along these shores. Enthusiasm ran high for this new way of relating to the Bay.

"Next morning while the boats were gassing up, I took some students into an adjoining field where we gathered poke (*Phytolacca americana*), dock (*Rumex crispus*), cleavers (*Galium aparine*), dandelion greens (*Taraxacum officinale*) and a host of other wild spring vegetables. Then out on the bright water of Piankatank River, we skimmed up to a beautiful, uninhabited island covered with groves of persimmon and pine.

"We had been warned that this tidal inlet offered no shellfish, but barely had we gotten ashore when we saw that the saltmarsh was alive with striated mussels (*Modiolus demissus*) and marsh periwinkle (*Littorina irrorata*). Although neither of these creatures is commonly eaten, both can furnish wholesome food to those not allergic to mulluscan shellfish. We gathered a supply. Cat-brier or green-brier (*Smilax rotundifolia*) was all too plentiful in the brushy parts of the island. New sprouts and leaf buds furnished a wild salad that was highly appreciated by the young foragers. There was more poke around abandoned camp sites, and along the trails we found all the sheep sorrel (*Rumex acetosella*) we could use. Our food hoard grew.

Royal Fern, one of the many edible wild plants available to the venturesome forager of the Bay Country. M.E. Warren

"We added various wild greens to our sandwich lunch, then headed for the adjacent mainland to do some exploring. There we found some of the same seaside plants I have enjoyed on the Maine Coast: sea rocket (*Cakile edentula*) and orach (*Atriplex patula*). A walk up in the fields gave us all the winter-cress (*Barbarea vulgaris*) we cared to gather besides furnishing more poke, dock, and other spring greens. Returning through the woods we found the angelica tree (*Aralia spinosa*), commonly called devil's walking-stick or Hercules' club, in great abundance. This spiny shrub grows a great panicle of large, compound leaves every spring. I had long heard that these leaves were edible if caught in exactly the right stage—when just unrolling, with the prickles still soft and tender—but this was the first time I had ever found them in that condition. So we helped ourselves to a good supply. They had a pleasant, aromatic flavor raw and gave promise of being a good vegetable cooked. A member of the famous ginseng family so highly valued by the Orientals, this shrub is supposed to restore lost youth and lengthen life. I needed a good shot of it, for these energetic youngsters were running me ragged.

"We followed a trail through the woods and came on the ruins of a great antebellum plantation headquarters. A magnificent mansion was falling apart, its roof and floors gone and a great patch of poke growing before the ornate fireplace in the huge living room. There were sunken gardens, overgrown box hedges and other signs of luxurious and opulent living now long vanished. In a little, brick-walled, family grave yard we found tombstones dating back to long before the Revolution.

"Amid all this faded glory a myriad of wild food plants grew in great abundance. We gathered more poke and winter-cress and dug a great supply of burdock roots (*Arctium minus*). A vegetable highly valued by the Japanese, burdock is another food that's supposed to revivify the old, refresh the tired, restore the energyless and fortify the weak. Scraped and cut crosswise like carrots, then boiled until tender and seasoned with butter and salt, they do make a good, starchy, potato like food.

"The lower end of a sunken garden had become marshy and grown up in cattails. We peeled the young stalks to get the tender hearts—so good in salads or boiled as a mild, sweet vegetable. We also dug a bagful of sassafras roots to make tea for the wild party we were planning.

"All day long we had tried to convince somebody to go fishing for some protein food to complement our wild vegetables. But everyone was so turned-on with wild food gathering that they refused to stop for anything so mundane as ordinary angling. When we first landed on the mainland I had noticed that the shallow bottom was covered with razor clam shells (*Tagelus gibbus*), so upon returning to the boats I suggested that we try to capture some of the live ones. The stout razor doesn't ust lie still and let you dig him up as a respectable edible clam is supposed to do. He lives in a burrow which he can quickly slide down until out of reach, and if you try digging down to him he simply escapes through the sand.

"But these smart youngsters soon proved capable of outwitting wily clams by suddenly thrusting one hand down into the sand and holding their victims still until they could dig them out with the other hand. These are delicious clams and we soon had enough to make a difference in the wild meal we were planning. However these young people were having too much fun to stop and the sun went down before they had their fill of this activity. We returned to the island laden with a wealth of wild food."

If Gibbons can't sell you on foraging the Chesapeake, no one can!

Learning from the Experts

Now I am really going to stick my neck out by encouraging non-scientists to play with scientific tools; more precisely, to use a system developed by scientists for scientists to comprehensively inventory the biota of the Chesapeake. I know what that suggests to some—darn-fool meddling in matters best left to experts. But I for one feel strongly about what should be left entirely to experts—in a word, nothing! I have been able to gain a better understanding of the Bay community through clumsy attempts to measure salinity, pH and dissolved oxygen. I've been on hand to see what happens when a teenager first discovers zooplankton—the incredulous "look-guys, they're-alive" reaction. So another step in the same direction—the one hereafter presented—is all of a piece.

The system I favor and present comes from a bookmark publication, one to which future generations of Chesapeake devotees will often refer. It is the before-mentioned Volume 13, Supplement to *Chesapeake Science*. *Chesapeake Science* is normally a quarterly journal published by the Natural Resources Institute of the University of Maryland. Volume 13, Supplement, December 1972 is a special Chesapeake Research Consortium Publication. As stated in a Preface by L. Eugene Cronin, Research Professor and Director of The Natural Resources Institute; David Challinor, Assistant Secretary for Science, Smithsonian Institution, and William J. Hargis, Jr., Director of the Virginia Institute of Marine Science, the Supplement provides "the first comprehensive summary of biota for the largest and most valuable estuarine system in the United States and will serve as a base line to guide future efforts and measure progress."

To realize such a goal, the Supplement editors requested and received from 26 specialists "a precis of the state of knowledge within their area of interest." Each summary follows an outline consisting of five parts.

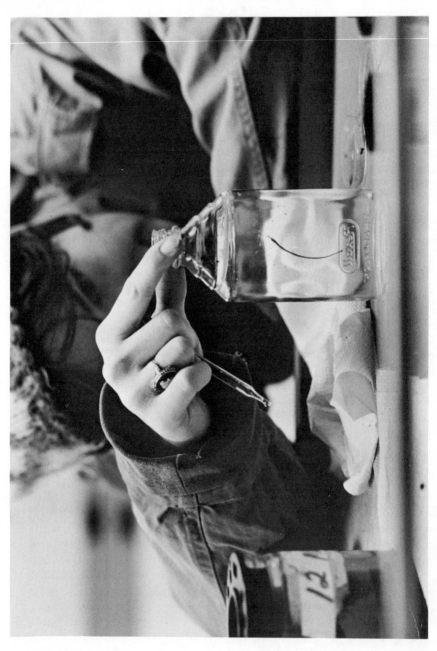

I've been on hand to see what happens when a teenager first discovers zooplankton—the incredulous "look-guys, they're-alive" reaction shown here. M.E. Warren

Each part is, in effect, the highly important right question to ask if one is attempting to establish the existing conditions—the present facts of life—about any one of the estimated 2,650 species of bacteria, parasites, and other plants and animals which make up the biota of the Chesapeake. Use of this outline can and should enable many of us with special interests of our own to keep a better record of our observations

If we know what to look for, we can find data of scientific significance. Here (l. to r.) Lance Miyamoto, Richie Blue, Denny Hayden, and Wendy Leigh test the salinity of Meredith Creek. A.W. Sherwood

in the field. It may also enable us to contribute significant new data scientifically important. As the Supplement editors note, the summaries submitted are "presented altogether as *an estimate of the current state of the art*. Such a composite allows areas of 'amazing ignorance' to be quickly assayed." (Emphasis mine.) If we know what to look for, surely the artist in all of us, the latent scientist in some of us, will respond to a challenge so appealing to both.

PART ONE OF THE OUTLINE: IDENTIFYING AND CLASSIFYING (NAMING) THE SPECIES IN QUESTION

For waterfowl of the Chesapeake Bay, contributor Robert E. Stewart lists six subfamilies: (1) Swans, (2) Geese, (3) Surface-feeding Ducks, (4) Diving Ducks, (5) Stiff-tailed Ducks, and (6) Mergansers; one specie of Swans: (1) Whistling Swan; two species of Geese: (1) Canada Goose, (2) Brant; nine species of Surface-feeding Ducks: (1) Mallard, (2) Black Duck, (3) Gadwall, (4) Pintail, (5) Green-winged Teal, (6) Blue-winged Teal, (7) American Widgeon, (8) Shoveler, (9) Wood Duck; eleven species of Diving Ducks: (1) Redhead, (2) Ringnecked Duck, (3) Canvasback, (4) Greater Scaup, (5) Lesser Scaup, (6) Common Goldeneye, (7) Bufflehead, (8) Oldsquaw, (9) Whitewinged Scoter, (10) Surf Scoter, (11) Common Scoter; one specie of Stiff-tailed Ducks: (1) Ruddy Duck; and three species of Mergansers: (1) Hooded Merganser, (2) Common Merganser, (3) Red-breasted Merganser.

In addition to the above, according to Stewart, the Snow Goose, Blue Goose, and European Widgeon are "rare or irregular" in the Chesapeake area, and a new subspecies of Blue-winged Teal has been reported.

With the benefit of an occasional winter weekend on the Bay with Hopkins ecologist William Sladen, I can add to that list. The Mute Swan has also been descried, particularly in and around the Miles River. Dr. Sladen tells me the Mute was introduced by Peter Thompson into Leeds Creek about ten years ago and that it has bred itself up to over 60 birds. Since the Mute stays around all year and is a voracious eater of aquatic grasses favored by the Whistlers, ducks, and geese, and since it is not a native bird, there is serious question as to whether it should be left alone to breed up to hundreds, perhaps thousands, and spread throughout the region.

To keep our own taxonomical (classification) list of waterfowl, all we need is one of the many excellent identification books (see Resource Reading) available; a good pair of binoculars; the American Ornithologists' Union Check-list of North American Birds; and the will—this the most important part of the equipment—to get off alone into the wilds of the Chesapeake with enough curiosity to know more about its waterfowl than we can possibly learn from books. Much the same kind of equipment, with the addition of nets and magnifying glasses as needed, would serve us equally well whether our interest is in snakes, salamanders, fishes, crabs, minute crustaceans, oysters, clams, mussels, parasites, worms, nettles, jellyfish, aquatic plants, algae, plankton, mushrooms, microorganisms, or trees—the good guys and the bad guys (sea nettles, oyster bores) which constitute the natural life of the Bay. Already demonstrated here in this one example of a specie not mentioned (the Mute Swan) is the fun of discovery implicit in every attempt to identify a specie in the field and to positively group it in its appropriate scientific classification. No scientist worth his degree will ever pooh-pooh a relevant find!

While you are out looking for waterfowl, keep an eye peeled for one of the 75 species and 22 families of birds, other than waterfowl, which are "characteristic inhabitants of regular occurrence on one or more

A saucy pair of Mallards, one of the nine species of surface-feeding ducks found on the Chesapeake. M.E. Warren

habitats of the Chesapeake Bay during appropriate seasons of the year."
Stewart's list includes loons (2 species); grebes (3 species); gannets (1
specie); cormorants (1 specie); herons (9 species); hawks and eagles (3
species); ospreys (1 specie); falcons (2 species); rails and coots (7
species); plovers and turnstones (4 species); snipe, sandpipers, etc. (13
species); gulls and terns (11 species); barn owls (1 specie); typical owls
(1 specie); kingfishers (1 specie); swallows (2 species); crows (2 species);
wrens (2 species); pipits (1 specie); wood warblers (1 specie); blackbirds, etc. (3 species); and sparrows (4 species).

PART TWO OF THE OUTLINE: EVALUATING THE SENSITIVITY OF THE SPECIES TO MAN-INDUCED ENVIRONMENTAL CHANGES

Stewart's evaluation of man's influence on Bay waterfowl may not
agree with your own, particularly if you are a hunter or fisherman, but
it provides an excellent example of what all of us should be thinking
about as we use—and unconsciously, perhaps, abuse—the resources of
the Bay.

In Stewart's opinion, "the quality of habitat (for waterfowl) has
deteriorated greatly during recent years." Contributing factors include
"pollution and increasing turbidity of fresh and slightly brackish
estuarine waters; encroachment of pest plants and animals, including
the waterchestnut, Eurasian watermilfoil, and carp; use of marshes and
other tide-water habitats for spoil and trash disposal, and the commercial development of these so-called 'waste' lands; ditching of
marshes for mosquito control; and destruction of beds of submerged
aquatic plants through clam-dredging operations, or by more direct
control measures designed to improve areas for swimming and boating.
Further destruction or impairment of waterfowl habitat must be halted
if further reduction in use of Chesapeake Bay by waterfowl is to be
avoided.

"Human disturbance reduces use by waterfowl in certain areas that
otherwise are suitable. Heavy hunting pressure, in particular, often has a
deleterious effect in this regard. Disturbance caused by speed boats
used for recreation, commercial fishing vessels, or large concentrations
of other boats frighten waterfowl from an area. Artillery firing, target
bombing, and low-flying planes and helicopters also reduce waterfowl
use. Waterfowl of open-water bays, sounds, and estuaries are especially
influenced by hunting, fishing, boating, and similar human activities."

Whether you agree with this analysis or not, can you doubt for a
moment how essential it is for all of us to undergo whatever mental
strain or stress it takes to make up our own minds as to what we and
our friends are doing to the resources of the Bay? Stewart's report
reminds me of a banding expedition, a CBF field trip, I participated in
last winter. We trapped 40 or 50 canvasbacks in West River. When I
think of a canvasback, I think of a premier bird for the table—fat, grain

nd grass-fed; delicious. The birds we handled were starved. Their breastbones stuck out like the edge of a knife. When released, they were unable to fly.

This peaceful scene on the Piankatank River is misleading. The quality of habitat for waterfowl is deteriorating. These decoys may see little service in the years ahead. M.E. Warren

I am also reminded of the sinking feeling I have these days when I hear about the increasingly popular sea duck (Scoter) shooting. Left alone for the sailor to enjoy while better birds were available, they are now considered good sport for the hunter—and the limit is seven birds per person per day during the season. I have known a sea duck to stay with a sailboat all day, as if the duck had found a playmate and the

boat a companion. It is impossible for me to accept the argument that
there are "plenty of them" and "it does 'em good to be weeded out.'

But not all the news is bad. Dr. Stewart will be glad to know that
over on the Shore, at Hambleton Island, an ingenious group, largely
volunteers, are proving that an indispensable food source for waterfowl—tidal marshes—can be planted anew. Dr. Edgar Garbisch is in
charge. If he and his co-workers are as successful as it appears they will
be, new marshes will be effective in controlling erosion and waterfowl
will have an important new source of food.

Dr. Edgar Garbisch (right) and Arthur Sherwood, CBF Director, are shown on
their way to Hambleton Island, Broad Creek. Frank Davis

PART THREE OF THE OUTLINE: DETERMINING THE
DISTRIBUTION AND ABUNDANCE OF THE SPECIES

When you take the time (and enjoy the fun) of helping to determine he distribution and abundance of a specie, what are you accomplishing? A mere exercise in statistical analysis? Absolutely not! Consider the following case histories reported by Dr. William Sladen.

(1) In August 1971, a small sample of only 10 adult (or sub-adult) swans were neck-collared (blue) by John Moore, Angus Gavin, Tom Gordon and myself in the Prudhoe Bay and Arctic National Wildlife Range part of Alaska's Northern slope. During the winter, 1971-72, we resighted (some of them many times) 8 of these 10 in Md, Va, or NC. This 80 percent resighting is quite remarkable when you consider these birds had safely travelled over 4,500 miles to their winter quarters and are still alive for continued observations. A pair of these were observed by Bowdy Train throughout the winter of 1971-72.

(2) Whistling Swans C030 and C031 (black neck collars) were neck-collared by John Moore in February 1970 in the Rhode River, south of Annapolis, Md. from John Colhoun's property at Ivy Neck. Before they left Maryland in March we had evidence that they were a pair. C030 was seen on the western shore of the Chesapeake Bay (Rhode River and Severn River) between November 1970 and 31 January 1971, whereas her mate, C031, was resighted between 26 December 1970 and 16 January 1971 by our colleague William Gelston at Boardman Lake, Traverse City, Michigan. So part of the winter 70-71 this pair was separated, the male spending some time in Michigan—by the way—with a large flock of Mute Swans.

We don't know where this pair is breeding in the Arctic (yet) but they were back together at Boardman Lake, Michigan on 4 December 1971 and remained there together all winter until they departed on spring migration on 6 April 1972.

Our latest information from Bill Gelston is that they returned to Boardman Lake again this fall on 9 November 1972 with 2 cygnets. Several interesting biological facts have come from these neck collars.

(a) They were separated for at least a part of the 1970-71 winter. Or was it that they had not yet established a permanent pair bond?

(b) They were together in Michigan all 1971-72 winter.

(c) C031 is about to spend (at least part of) a third consecutive winter and C030 a second in Michigan. Thus we must record Michigan as a regular wintering place for some of our eastern Whistlers.

(d) This pair gives us further evidence that neck collars are not deterring Whistlers from mating or rearing cygnets.

Dr. William Sladen and associates are exhaustively studying the Whistling Swan. A pair is shown here in Tilghman Creek, near Rich Neck Manor. M.E. Warren

That is how specific you can be when you count species. To make your field research as meaningful as possible, you will want to obtain as much background information as you can. In most instances, valuable resource information is available. For the following summary of the "present status of knowledge about the distribution and abundance" of waterfowl of the Chesapeake, Stewart lists 21 reference works, all of which are available.

"Chesapeake Bay is the chief focal point along the Atlantic coast for vast numbers of migrating waterfowl. Wintering populations also are of considerable importance. For a few species, the area often contains the largest wintering concentrations in North America. These include the Whistling Swan, Canada Goose, Black Duck, and Canvasback. Very large numbers of American Widgeon, Redheads, Lesser Scaup and Ruddy Ducks usually winter here also. The rather limited breeding populations, represented chiefly by the Black Duck, are largely restricted to local areas along the eastern shore of the Bay.

"The greatest concentrations of transient and wintering waterfowl occur along the central eastern shore of Chesapeake Bay in the Chester River, Eastern Bay, and Choptank River sections. Brackish estuarine bays with large, adjoining agricultural fields are the principal waterfowl habitats in these sections. During some years, the Blackwater-Nanticoke section, which contains extensive fresh and brackish estuarine marshes, also attracts large numbers of waterfowl. The Susquehanna Flats, with their luxuriant beds of fresh-water submerged plants, were one of the principal concentration areas during the spring and fall migration periods. Fairly large populations usually are present in the various habitat combinations that occur in other portions of Chesapeake Bay or adjoining estuaries."

PART FOUR OF THE OUTLINE: THE BIOLOGY OF THE SPECIES

Since the sex life of your plant or animal is a major part of its biology, the boning up in this area can be comfortable winter's work.

As an example of what to expect, consider the love life of an oyster. Male and female lie on the same "bed" or "bar," though not necessarily, and not usually, together. When conditions are just right, the right salinity, the right temperature, etc., they sexually stimulate one another by a kind of chemical extrusion—an extract of oyster, one supposes, that has the seductiveness, if not the properties, of oyster perfume. Moved by cooperative currents and tides, the extrusion of oyster activates the male sperm (trillions of cells) and the female eggs (millions). Released into the water, the cells meet, if they meet at all, in a floating milky way. Soon thereafter a few impregnated eggs—now oyster larvae—find their way back to a hard bottom and fix themselves thereon for life.

Or consider the popular love life of crabs—a very sexy species by any measure. Observing "doublers" swimming about in the upper Bay in late summer, you probably assumed you were seeing the real thing. Wrong. You were witnessing a preliminary part of an intricate process.

Oyster dredging out of Crisfield from the deck of a skipjack. The biology of this favorite Bay delicacy is a fascinating subject. The Baltimore *Sun*

It begins when a male is attracted to a virgin ready to shed her shell (moult) for the last time. Still a hard crab, she nevertheless submits to being approached, secured and carried away by an aggressive male. He takes her to a favorite moulting ground, sometimes miles away. There, in warm, shallow, protected water, defended by her mate, she completes her moult. She is now a soft crab—ready and willing to be mounted and impregnated through her two genital openings. (The male has corresponding appendages.) A day or two after intercourse, the female is hard again and able to travel. She swims south to the lower Bay, hibernates in mud for the winter, and spawns the following spring.

Stewart's comments on the biology of waterfowl are brief, and simply alert us to an extensive bibliography on the subject. For most Bay species you might choose to study, there is comparable material available.

PART FIVE OF THE OUTLINE:
THE ROLE OF THE SPECIES IN THE BAY ECOSYSTEM

What this boils down to is a matter of eating—what eats the specie and what the specie eats. Stewart gives the following account of the feeding habits of Bay waterfowl.

"Food habits of waterfowl on the Chesapeake Bay and adjoining estuaries vary greatly from one species to another, from one habitat to another, and also are influenced by seasonal changes in availability of foods. For the majority of waterfowl, widgeongrass (*Ruppia maritima*) probably is the most important single food item. Corn, either as waste grain in agricultural fields or as illegal bait in tidewater habitats is an important food for many kinds of waterfowl. Other food plants that are commonly used, at least locally, include wild celery (*Vallisneria americana*), eelgrass (*Zostera marine*), Olney three-square (*Scirpus olneyi*), and dotted smartweed (*Polygonum punctatum*). The more important animal foods in the region are the bivalve Baltic macoma (*Macoma balthica*), the little surf clam (*Mulinia lateralis*), the saltmarsh snail (*Melampus bidentatus*), various tiny gastropod mollusks (including *Littoridinops sp.*, *Bittium sp.*, and *Actecina canaliculata*), amphipod crustaceans (*Gammaridae*), mud crabs (*Xanthidae*), and midge larvae (*Chironomidae*)."

Bay waterfowl, Stewart reports, are subject to three kinds of predation. They are favorite sport for hunters; they are preyed upon by fox, mink, otter, raccoon, hawks and owls; during spring and early summer, the eggs of Eastern Shore breeding ducks are relished by crows, gulls, raccoons, skunks, and pilot black snakes.

There it is—a simple blueprint for getting to know more about the animals and plants of the Bay than you know now. Just that; nothing more, nothing less. What Robert E. Stewart did in his summary is the

For a few species of waterfowl, including the Canada Goose shown here at Remington Farms, the Chesapeake "often contains the largest wintering concentration in North America." M.E. Warren

work of a professional. I quote extensively from him to give you a case history of how each part of the five-part outline should be treated. Those of us who are not experts cannot expect to find instant success as an amateur botanist, biologist, or ecologist, but we can and we must do more than we have done till now to base our values and judgments (and our votes) on firsthand experiences.

There is no magic to finding, identifying, counting, observing, and reading about Bay biota; the magic is in the mind as it absorbs our experience and begins to work on our conscience.

A section of South Marsh Island. Tidal marshes are an important food source for waterfowl and an essential link in the relatively short and vulnerable food chain of the Bay. The Baltimore *Sun*

The Bay is the largest and most valuable estuarine system in the world. Here, pound net fishermen help prove the point. M.E. Warren

IX. CONCLUSION

I am often asked one or another or all of the following three questions:
    (1) Isn't it frustrating to work on the Bay as a conservationist?
    (2) What is hurting the Bay most?
    (3) Isn't the problem really people?

My easy answer to Question One is *No.* I find it a delight. By and large reasonably informed, interesting people are on the side of today's conservationist, provided the type is not defined too narrowly. I don't.

tterley, a working plantation overlooking the Patuxent River. Allies in the cause of nservation are those willing to get out-of-doors to appreciate Chesapeake country like this. M.E. Warren

I count as allies those who may be found, on occasion, out under an open sky, long enough divorced from TV and kindred diversions to appreciate the scenery with normal sensitivity. It is a wonder how little of Thoreau there is in most of us, and how little, thank God, is needed.

Lack of accomplishment may appear to dampen the spirits of conservationists, and I am sure it does at times. Even the bounciest spirits slide a while when evidence of an oil spill or a new development on the Bay or another fish kill appears on the record. But those of us who think of ourselves as workers rather than saviours don't pitch our expectations to saving the Bay all at once, or by ourselves, and, therefore, we refrain from writhing in failure with more than ordinary frustration.

Question Two gives me more trouble. My answer necessarily depends largely on secondhand sources. As I hear it, see it, the thing that is

People are an environmental hazard when they contribute to uncontrolled growth and community sprawl, the "chaos" which unavoidably pollutes as it proliferates. The example of sprawl is adjacent to Northern Parkway, Baltimore County. M.E. Warren

hurting most, right now, is insufficiently treated sewage entering the Bay and its tributaries—artificially induced eutrophication.

Tertiary treatment is very rare. Even the best secondary system discharges amounts of phosphates and nitrates. These combine to over-enrich the receiving waters, causing calamitous algae blooms. The end result is water deprived of an adequate supply of oxygen.

For too many years, we have tended to consider the Bay a convenient place to dump our "waste."

We know, now, there is no such thing as waste—that "everything must go somewhere."

We know that "everything is connected to everything else"—that the Bay environment is an ecological unit.

We know we cannot rob Peter to pay Paul environmentally—that "there's no such thing as a free lunch."

We know that a natural system like the Bay has limited tolerance for unnatural toying with it—"that nature knows best."

We know, in short, that the "laws of ecology" are considerably more inflexible than man-made laws; that we continue to pour insufficiently treated sewage into the Bay with a recklessness that ill suits us.

To Question Three my answer is mixed. Yes, when people contribute to uncontrolled growth and community sprawl, the "chaos" which unavoidably pollutes as it proliferates; No, when they accept their unique responsibilities as men.

"If the people packed up and left the Chesapeake Bay alone with its shellfish and finfish and plankton and birds and beautiful sky and rugged waters and marshland and all the wild creatures that live in its environs; if the Bay was allowed to return to nature 100 percent—in the course of some hundreds of years it would cease to exist. Siltation and erosion would fill it in and it would become the world's largest mud pie." To those accustomed to downgrade man's role in the evolution of the Chesapeake estuarine system, this must be a startling idea. It was recently presented by Hal Willard in a series of articles on the Bay. He wrote for the *Washington Post* and represents the thinking of Dr. Donald W. Pritchard. In his own words, Pritchard says: "We are living in what could be called the Age of Estuaries. For x number of centuries there were no estuaries. Now there are estuaries, primarily because of the glaciers. If there were no human beings to maintain them, in x number of centuries there would be no estuaries."

In my book, that is good news; it's nice to be needed. Man—a necessary component part of the Bay environment—has a responsibility to sustain it as he uses it. If we compete for its riches, we will probably soon exhaust them. But if we care for them with an awareness of their interdependence—with the awareness of a "whole man"—I venture to say the future prospects for the Bay are bright.

The Miles River, with St. Michaels in the foreground. If we care for the resources of the Bay with an awareness of their interdependence, the future prospects for the Bay are bright. M.E. Warren

KEY FACTS AND FIGURES

These sailors are conservationists, whether they know it or not! Frank Lawson

KEY FACTS AND FIGURES

Population and Projected Growth

The population of the region in 1960 was 11 million; in 1970, 15 million; by 2020 it is estimated the population will reach 30 million. The 50-year projection, 1970-2020, suggests "chaos" to Robert T. Dennis, formerly Director of Central Atlantic Environment Service: "uncontrolled growth, community sprawl, industrial locations determined by economic factors more than anything else, creeping pollution, declining quality of life for all of us."

Current Problems Affecting the Bay

Dr. William Donald Pritchard, Director of the Chesapeake Bay Institute at the Johns Hopkins University and a CBF trustee, ranks sewage and eutrophication, oil spillage, waste and resource consumption by heavy industry, sediment, chemical killers (pesticides, etc.), litter, light industry, dredging spoil, engineering works, fossil power, and nuclear power, in that order, as problems affecting the Bay and its resources. Fourteen principal trouble spots have been identified by the Chesapeake Research Consortium.

Bay Harvest

L. Eugene Cronin, Director of the Natural Resources Institute of the University of Maryland and a CBF Trustee, estimates that half a billion pounds of seafood is currently harvested from the Chesapeake annually. Commercial landings for 1971:

	Maryland		Virginia	
	Lbs.	Dollars	Lbs.	Dollars
Finfish including:	16,174,343	$ 1,714,800	50,596,176	$3,049,559
Menhaden	5,957,567	119,294	18,520,644	213,297
Striped Bass	2,743,007	861,892	1,183,356	280,140
Bluefish	140,981	14,991	610,970	61,572
Flounder	313,695	102,998	1,780,352	524,169
Shad	946,631	123,020		
White Perch	1,507,706	240,144		
Blue Crabs	27,605,979	3,201,463	48,440,541	4,008,422
Hard Clam Meats	332,131	192,089	1,836,544	1,397,837
Soft Clam Meats	5,986,120	2,993,064		
Surf Clam Meats	7,751,436	980,736	4,506,622	526,715
Oyster Meats	17,131,100	10,693,640	8,322,608	5,341,321

Much of the Bay is subject to exploitation as a "commons."

Bay Commercial Development

Billions of dollars worth of commercial installations are concentrated in and around Baltimore and Norfolk, substantiating the claim that the resources of the Bay can be progressively developed without punishing the overall character of the Bay. Cluster development will take continued recognition that there is room for all and a right place for each. It will require businessmen who possess enough breadth of vision to combine highly refined acquisitive instincts with a gut feeling for the precariousness of natural resources.

Vital Statistics

"The Chesapeake Bay is the crown jewel of the 850 estuaries and bays along the several coasts of the United States. It is the largest bay in the country, more valuable for human uses than any other estuary, and vulnerable to destruction from human use and abuse." The total drainage area of the Bay is 64,000 square miles, the size of the state of Washington. It is 200 miles long; an average of 15 miles wide; 5,000 miles of tidewater shoreline; 4,300 square miles of surface water; an average depth of 21 feet; receiving fresh water from over 150 major tributaries. The Susquehanna alone produces a mean discharge of 40,000 cubic feet per second of fresh water into the Bay.

The Bay's Ecological Unity and Dynamic Character

Geologist-Geographer Markley Gordon Wolman emphasizes the significance of the Bay's ecological unity and dynamic character. An example of the ecological unity of the Bay is the fact that the blue crab spawns in the lower bay and breeds in the upper bay. Examples of the dynamic character of the Bay are its rate of erosion and sedimentation. Four hundred and fifty acres of Sharps Island eroded away to nothing within 100 years. Eight million tons of sediment flow into the Bay per year.

Geologic History

The Bay's "geologic history is imminent." The Bay is a relatively new and young environment, not more than eight to ten thousand years old, the result of the last glacial melting which flooded the Susquehanna River Valley. "The so-called 'natural' scene is, in this region, neither static nor even ponderous in its rate of movement."

A Partially Mixed Estuary

An estuary is a coastal body of water open to the sea within which sea water is measurably diluted by fresh water drainage from the land. As oceanographer (and CBF trustee) William Donald Pritchard explains, the Bay is a partially mixed estuary "because the salinity distribution, while showing an increase with depth, indicating the estuary is not completely mixed vertically, does not show sharp boundary separating an upper, low salinity layer from an intruding wedge-shaped bottom layer of high salinity, which is characteristic of a class of estuaries having small tidal currents, and which are called salt wedge estuaries." The Bay is fortunate in having a circulation of fresh and salt water which gives it a daily cleaning.

A Short Vulnerable Food Chain

Because the Chesapeake estuarine system is geologically young and dynamic, and because it is a comparatively rare ecosystem, living organisms of the area have had to make major adaptions in a relatively short time (8 to 10 thousand years). Not many species have so adapted. The Bay has, therefore, what is considered a "short" food chain. Since any one of a relatively few species is more dependent upon another than if a larger choice were available, the food chain as a whole is particularly vulnerable to damage. Biologically speaking, the fauna and flora of the Bay live a precarious existence.

Bay Inventory

(1) Producers—plants
   a. Marshes
   b. Submerged aquatics
   c. Phytoplankton (microscopic drifting plants)
(2) Consumers—animals
   a. Bottom, including crab, oyster, clam
   b. Drifters, larval stage of most Bay animals—zooplankton
   c. Swimmers, resident (rockfish); spawners (shad); visitors (bluefish)
   d. Birds, mammals and reptiles

Man—A Necessary Component Part of the Bay System

"We are living in what could be called the Age of Estuaries. For x number of centuries there were no estuaries. Now there are estuaries, primarily because of the glaciers. If there were no human beings to maintain them, in x number of years there would be no estuaries." Man, obviously a necessary component part of the Bay environment, has the responsibility to sustain it as he uses it.

Early History

CBF Assistant Director H.K. Rigg contributes the following account.

Some historians believe that Thorfinn Karlsefni, a Viking explorer, discovered the Bay while sailing his ship along the East coast of North America in the eleventh century—approximately 500 years before Columbus reached the New World. Others place credence in the tales of Brendan, an Irish saint and sailor. Ancient sagas mention the saint as having sailed the Atlantic in a coracle, or hide-covered boat, and discovering the Bay region in about the sixth century.

Nothing definitive is known about the history of the Chesapeake Bay until Indian settlements were formed along its shores. The Choptank, Nanticoke, Susquehannock and Assateague tribes were probably the first permanent inhabitants of the area. In fact, the name "Chesapeake" is an Indian word which has been variously interpreted as meaning, "highly salted body of water," "mother of waters," "great shellfish bay," and "country on great water."

Probably the first white men to explore the Chesapeake Bay were a group of Spaniards led by Vincente Gonzales who served under Governor Mendenez of the Spanish colony in St. Augustine, Florida in 1588. Captain Gonzales' mission was to determine if the English had a base in the Bay region. After entering the Capes, Gonzales coasted along the western shore all the way up to the mouth of the Susquehanna and returned following the eastern shoreline, accurately describing the islands he encountered. Unfortunately, he left no charts of his voyage.

In 1606, Captain John Smith, of the Jamestown colony, conducted an organized exploration of the Chesapeake. For 60 days, he and a few companions sailed the Bay's waters as far as the mouth of the Susquehanna in search of precious metals and the Northwest Passage.

After their return to Jamestown, Smith drew a map of the territory. This first known map of the Chesapeake was published in England in 1612, and for nearly a century it served as the principal navigational chart of the Bay.

Sport Fishing and Sailing

The Bay is a recreational paradise. River sailing and hundreds of pleasant safe anchorages make it the finest cruising ground in the world. CBF Assistant Director William Mullins contributes the following comments on sport fishing.

Sport fishing on the Chesapeake Bay is more than an avocation—it is a way of life. Blessed with resources that are both bountiful and accessible, Bay country residents annually haul out a sport fishing catch that matches the commercial catch in weight and value.

Rockfish (the local name for striped bass) and bluefish are the aristocrats of the Bay. Both are highly prized as fighters and table fare. Rock are year-round residents of the Bay and in plentiful supply from the Susquehanna Flats to the Virginia Capes. The current Bay record is held by a 50 pounder; fish weighing 15 to 30 pounds are not uncommon.

Blues invade the Bay in late spring and remain in residence until early fall. Rarely, however, do they travel north of the Bay Bridge. Noted for their voracious appetites, a hungry blue will sink his sharp teeth into almost anything that moves. Chesapeake blues are of a smaller size than the ocean travellers, but an occasional 10 pounder keeps the angler on his toes. Rock and bluefish are caught by trolling, casting, chumming and drifting.

White perch and spot are common Bay fish highly regarded for their food value. Both are widely distributed throughout the Bay although the spot are available only in summer. The common method for catching both species is bottom fishing with bloodworms or similar bait.

The higher salinity of the lower Bay attracts saltwater species such as sea trout, flounder, cobia, and channel bass. Seasonal runs of shad, yellow perch, pickerel occur throughout the Bay and offer the angling enthusiast year-round sport. Those interested in pursuing sport fishing in Bay waters should buy one of the many excellent books available in tackle shops or write to state fishing departments in Richmond and Annapolis for free information.

The Parallel Chesapeake Bay Bridge . . . a towering symbol of regional growth, it challenges the Chesapeake Community to plan for, rather than succumb to, inevitable development. M.E. Warren

BIBLIOGRAPHY

BIBLIOGRAPHY

(I comment on the books which have been most helpful to me. Others are included because I think they contribute to a useful bibliography on the Bay and to an understanding of estuaries. Technical books listed here supplement those included in the Resource Material of the Chesapeake Bay Foundation Cruise Guide, Appendix 1.)

Abbott, R. Tucker, *Sea Shells of the World,* 1962; the Golden Nature Series, Golden Press, New York

Barrie, George, Jr. and Robert Barrie, *Cruises—Mainly in the Bay of the Chesapeake,* 1909; The Franklin Press (The Barrie brothers and the Chesapeake enjoyed a life-long love affair, an important issue from which is this delightful account of cruising on the Bay.)

Beirne, Francis F., *The Amiable Baltimoreans,* 1951; E. P. Dutton & Co. Inc., New York
(What a gentle and beautiful man was Francis F. Beirne. He treats the Bay's largest city with taste, distinction, and infectious humor.)

Blair, Carvel Hall, with Willits Dyer Ansel, *Chesapeake Bay: Notes and Sketches,* 1970; Tidewater Publishers, Cambridge, Md.

Blanchard, Fessenden S., assisted by William T. Stone, *A Cruising Guide to the Chesapeake,* 1962; Dodd, Mead & Co., New York (William T. Stone has updated this excellent guide.)

Bodine, Aldine Aubrey, *Chesapeake Bay and Tidewater,* 1954; Bodine and Associates, Baltimore, Md.

Brewington, M. V., *Chesapeake Bay Sailing Craft,* 1966; Maryland Historical Society and Chesapeake Bay Maritime Museum

Brockman, C. Frank, *Trees of North America,* 1968; Golden Field Guide Series, Golden Press, New York

Brooks, Kenneth F., Jr., *Run to the Lee,* 1965; W. W. Norton & Co., Inc., New York

Brown, Alexander Crosby, *Steam Packets on the Chesapeake—A History of the Old Bay Line Since 1840,* 1961; Cornell Maritime Press, Inc., Cambridge, Md.

Burgess, Robert H., *This Was Chesapeake Bay,* 1963; Cornell Maritime Press, Inc., Cambridge, Md.
Chesapeake Circle, 1965; Cornell Maritime Press, Inc.
Coasting Captain—Journals of Captain Leonard S. Tawes, 1967; The Mariners Museum, Newport News, Va.
(Robert H. Burgess, curator of the Maritime Museum at Newport News, is a valued trustee and advisor to CBF. This journal beautifully evokes the character of Captain Tawes.)

Byron, Gilbert, *Early Explorations of the Chesapeake Bay,* 1960; Maryland Historical Society

Carter, George F., *A Study of Soils and Land Forms of the Chesapeake Bay Margins,* 1951; Johns Hopkins University, Baltimore, Md.

Chesapeake Bay Foundation, Inc., *We Need You,* 1973; Annual Report of the Chesapeake Bay Foundation, Inc., Annapolis, Md. (Available. Write CBF, "The Church," Prince George and East Sts., P. O. Box 1709, Annapolis, Md. 21404.)

Chesapeake-Potomac Study Commission. *Report on Fish and Shellfish in the Chesapeake Bay and Potomac River with Recommendations for Their Future Management,* 1948; Daily Record Company

Commoner, Barry, *The Closing Circle—Nature, Man and Technology,* 1971; Alfred A. Knopf, Inc., New York
(I have read *The Closing Circle* three times; I will read it again. Commoner is an exceptionally fine ecologist and an exceptionally effective teacher.)

Chesapeake Research Consortium, Inc. Annual Report. June 1, 1971–May 31, 1972. The Johns Hopkins University, University of Maryland, Smithsonian Institution, Virginia Institute of Marine Science

Cronin, Lewis Eugene, *The Condition of the Chesapeake Bay,* 1967; Wildlife Management Institute, Washington, D.C.

Davis, Deering, *Annapolis Houses 1700–1775,* 1957; Bonanza Books, New York

Earle, Swepson, *The Chesapeake Bay Country,* 1923; Thomsen-Ellis Company, Baltimore, Md.
(My devotion to this Chesapeake classic influenced my decision not to include a section on the great houses of the Bay and their histories. Go straight to Swepson Earle.)

Farragut, Paul R., *A Reconnaissance Study of the Chesapeake Bay,* 1968; For the Maryland Regional Planning Council

Footner, Hulbert, *Maryland Main and the Eastern Shore,* illustrated by Louis Ruyl, 1942; D. Appleton-Century Co. Inc., New York
Rivers of the Eastern Shore, illustrated by Aaron Sopher, 1944; reprinted by Tidewater Publishers, Cambridge, Md.
(If there were more accounts like this there might be more successful efforts made to preserve the priceless beauty of the rivers of the Eastern Shore. As I write this, plans are underway for the development of Wye Island. It makes me cringe.)

Gibbons, Euell, *Organic Gardening,* Vol. 19, No. 8, August, 1972; Published monthly by Rodale Press, Inc., Emmaus, Pa. (Euell Gibbons writes on a foraging expedition on the Bay. I was with him. He is a fabulous man.)

Hardin, Garret James, *Nature and Man's Fate,* 1959; NAL, New York
Science Conflict and Society, 1969

Hargis, William J., Jr., *Research on Chesapeake Bay and Contiguous Waters of the Chesapeake Bight of the Virginia Sea,* 1971; Virginia Institute of Marine Science, Gloucester, Va.

Hargis, William J., Jr., and M. P. Lynch, *Virginia State Agencies Concerned with Coastal Zone Planning, Management or Scientific and Engineering Activities,* 1971; Second edition, enlarged, Virginia Institute of Marine Science, Gloucester, Va.

Henderson, Richard, *Sail and Power—A Manual of Seamanship,* 1967; U. S. Naval Institute, Annapolis, Md.
Sea Sense, 1972; International Marine Publishing Co., Camden, Me. (Read Henderson if you want to know more about sailing, boats, and the sea.)

Hill, Norman Alan, *Chesapeake Cruise,* 1944; George W. King Printing Company

Hittman Associates, Inc. with Arthur W. Sherwood, *Proposal for an Analysis of Legal Problems Related to the Development and Management of Chesapeake Bay Resources,* 1968

Hotchkiss, Neil, *Common Marsh Plants of the United States and Canada,* December, 1970; Bureau of Sport Fisheries and Wildlife, U.S. Department of Interior

Kelly, F. Lines, *Citizen Participation in Protecting Bay Wetlands,* 1972; The Chesapeake Bay Foundation

Klingel, Gilbert C., *The Bay; A Naturalist Discovers a Universe of Life Above and Below the Chesapeake,* 1951; Dodd, Mead & Co., New York
(The subtitle accurately describes this book. I would like to have known Klingel while he was exploring the Bay. His book is fascinating. He uses the Bay to illustrate Emerson's idea that, "God reappears with all His parts in every moss and cobweb.")

Lang, Varley, *Follow the Water,* 1961; John F. Blair, Publisher, Winston-Salem, N.C.

Lasson, Kenneth L., *Historical Perspective, Extracted from Chesapeake Bay in Legal Perspective,* 1970; Natural Resources Institute, University of Maryland, Silver Springs, Md.

Latrobe, Ferdinand Claiborne, *Chesapeake Bay Cookbook,* 1956; Horn-Shafer

Leopold, Aldo, *A Sand County Almanac, and Sketches Here and There,* 1949; Oxford University Press, New York
(As a naturalist and a superb writer, Leopold has few peers.)

MacKenthun, Kenneth M., *The Practice of Water Pollution Biology*, 1969; U.S. Department of the Interior, Federal Water Pollution Control Administration, Division of Technical Support

Maloney, John, *Chesapeake Odyssey: An 18-foot Sailboat Follows the Course of Captain John Smith Around This Spacious Bay of History, Commerce, Sea Food, and Nautical Lore*, 1939; National Geographic Society, Washington, D.C.

Marsh, George Perkins, *Man and Nature; or, Physical Geography as Modified by Human Action*, 1864; C. Scribner & Company, reprinted by Harvard University Press, Cambridge, Ma.
(An exciting introduction to the study of the interrelationship of plants and animals. Marsh was an extraordinary man.)

Maryland-District of Columbia Meeting. *Clean Water. . .For the Nation's Estuaries. Proceedings of the Maryland-District of Columbia Public Meeting*, 2 Vols. 1968; Federal Water Pollution Administration, U. S. Department of Interior

Middleton, Arthur Pierce, *Tobacco Coast, A Maritime History of Chesapeake Bay in the Colonial Era*, 1953; The Mariners Museum, Newport News, Va.

Miers, Earl Schenck, *The Drowned River; The Story of the Chesapeake Bay; An Essay*, 1967; The Curtis Paper Company, Newark, De.

Mitchell, Carleton, *The Winds Call*, 1971; Charles Scribner's Sons, New York
Yachtsman's Camera, 1950; D. Van Nostrand Co. Inc., Princeton, N.J.

National Planning Association, *Summary Economic Base Study: Chesapeake Bay Drainage Basins*, 1967; Federal Water Pollution Control Administration

Natural Resources Institute of the University of Maryland, *Bay Biota*, Chesapeake Science, Vol. 13, Supplement—December 1972. A quarterly journal published by the National Resources Institute of the University of Maryland, Chesapeake Biological Laboratory, Solomons, Maryland. L. Eugene Cronin, Director.
(I repeat from my text: This is an important publication, bound to be used for years to come by all those who wish to refine their knowledge and awareness of Bay biota.)
Conference Report—Citizens Program for the Chesapeake Bay, 1971; University of Maryland, Natural Resources Institute, Silver Springs, Md.

Nobile, Philip and John Deedy, *The Complete Ecology Fact Book*, 1972; Doubleday and Company, Inc., Garden City, New York

Perkinson, William J., Bill Burton and Dean Mills, *The Chesapeake at Bay*, Baltimore Evening *Sun*, Publishers

ower, Garret and Daniel A. Bronstein, *Chesapeake Bay in Legal Perspective,* 1970; prepared by the University of Maryland Law School for the Department of Interior, Federal Water Pollution Control Administration
(One of a kind. Professor Power and students at the University of Maryland School of Law submitted a proposal and won. The work justifies their selection.)

Reid, George K., *Ecology of Inland Waters and Estuaries,* 1961; Van Nostrand Reinhold Company, Princeton, N.J.

Remande, Adolf and Carl Schlieper, *Biology of Brackish Water,* 1971; John Wiley & Sons, Inc., New York

Robbins, Chandler S., Bertel Bruun, and Herbert S. Zim, *Birds of North America,* 1966; Golden Field Guide Series, Golden Press, New York

Rothrock, J.T., *Vacation Cruising in Chesapeake and Delaware Bays,* 1884; J.B. Lippincott & Company, Philadelphia, Pa.
(One of the books I would choose to take with me to a desert island. Charming, instructive and entertaining. I am indebted for it to Dr. Roger P. Batchelor.)

Rudloe, Jack, *The Erotic Ocean, A Handbook for Beachcombers,* 1971; World Publishing Company, New York

Seitz, R. C., *Temperature and Salinity Distributions in Vertical Sections Along the Longitudinal Axis and Across the Entrance of the Chesapeake Bay (April 1968–March 1969),* 1971; Chesapeake Bay Institute, the Johns Hopkins University
(Important scientific work easy for the layman to understand and emulate.)

Semmes, Raphael, *Captains and Mariners of Early Maryland,* 1937; The Johns Hopkins Press, Baltimore, Md.
(Those interested in the early maritime history of the Bay will find this great fun.)

Shurtleff, Byron Parker, *Seeing the Chesapeake Wilds,* University of Delaware, Newark, De.

Skiruen, Percy G., *The First Parishes of the Province of Maryland,* 1923; Norman, Remington Company

State of Maryland, *Proceedings of the Governor's Conference on the Chesapeake Bay,* 1968
(Excellent reports were given at this conference by Drs. Hargis, Cronin, Pritchard, and Wolman.)
Catalog of Natural Areas in Maryland, 1968; State of Maryland Planning Department

Stegner, Robert W. and Val E. Arnsdorf, *A Sourcebook for Population–Environment Studies,* Experimental Edition, 1972; Population Curriculum Study, University of Delaware, Newark, De.

(I share the author's enthusiasm for an inter-disciplinary approach t
environmental education. I am one of their unregistered students.)

Suttor, Richard E., *The Commercial Fishing and Seafood Processin
Industries of the Chesapeake Bay Area,* 1968; University of Mary
land, Silver Springs, Md.

Tunis, Edwin, *Shaws Fortune, The Picture Story of a Colonial Planta
tion,* 1966; World Publishing Co., New York

Walsh, Roy, E., *Gunning the Chesapeake—Duck and Goose Shooting o*
the Eastern Shore, 1960; Tidewater Publishers, Cambridge, Md.
Sanctuary Pond—A Conversation Piece, 1967; Barre Publishers
Barre, Ma.

Wass and Wright, *Coastal Wetlands of Virginia,* 1969; VIMS

Weyl, Peter K., *Oceanography, An Introduction to the Marine Environ
ment,* 1970; John Wiley & Sons, New York

Wilstach, Paul, *Tidewater Maryland,* 1931; The Bobbs-Merrill Company
reprinted by Tidewater Publishers, Cambridge, Md.

APPENDIX

CBF Ecology Cruise Guide

by

James R. Howard III   John T. Gookin

Nancy G. Dimsdale   David K. Martin

John Page Williams, Jr.

CONTENTS

INTRODUCTION

A success story! This cruise guide, matured over a period of several years and substantially revised, is now in its fourth printing.

James R. Howard III, Chairman of the Department of Science at the Park School and a valued advisor to CBF, contributes a thoughtful analysis of water studies applicable to an estuarine system. The glossary is also his. Our own staff biologist, Nancy Dimsdale, adds comments and figures relating particular findings and measurements to average and healthy conditions. John Page Williams, Jr., presently a biology teacher at St. Christopher's School, Richmond, and soon-to-be CBF educational director, contributes a section on the pleasures of gunkholing along tidal shores and marshes. CBF Student Coordinators John Gookin and Dave Martin round out the presentation with practical descriptions of beach studies and instructions for the use and fabrication of simple, do-it-yourself ecological testing equipment.

The combined contributions present a set of instructions, guidelines, observations and information designed to be used as a *practical tool* for your better observation and understanding of the Chesapeake environment. We sincerely hope you, your family and friends, will use it.

Should anyone question his scientific ability and grow faint before such apparently taxing phrases as secchi disks and aerobic organisms, take heart! Prior to my becoming engulfed in the affairs of CBF, I thought myself a daring and ingenious fellow if I ventured the opinion, after careful scrutiny with a binocular, that I had sighted a Great Blue Heron. Unfortunately, I am not exaggerating. Now, having referred to this *Guide* many times (not always with exacting results), I can assure you I take my place at a LaMotte dissolved oxygen test kit with complete confidence.

So please don't put this Report aside with the thought, "It's not for me." *It is for you.* It was originally put together for use on our ecology cruises. But when we saw what fun and excitement, what a new dimension in enjoyment of the Bay the cruises opened up to skippers and their young crews, we redesigned the *Guide* to be used by anyone on the water or shore disposed to explore on his own.

Sensual enjoyment of an intriguing environment like the Bay is easy. It takes more—something like "work"—to cultivate an understanding of the system. It takes time and attention to learn to appreciate what "tends to preserve" its integrity, stability and beauty. We hope this *Guide* tempts you in that direction. If it does, we think it will help you contribute to the sound management of our natural resources.

Arthur W. Sherwood

93

SIGNIFICANCE OF WHAT YOU ARE GOING
TO BE DOING AND OBSERVING

During the time you spend studying and observing the Chesapeake Bay, you will learn many things. But you may well ask, how does this relate to me and to my community? Why should we study it? What can we find out that will be of lasting importance in our lives?

First of all, any time spent on the Chesapeake Bay will enrich your life, enlarge your understanding, and increase your appreciation of the natural areas that we are trying so hard to preserve. We hope it will inspire you to work with us in this effort.

For an in-depth understanding of the Chesapeake Bay, you need to know how the system works. What are the food webs, what are the habitat requirements, and what changes will occur or have occurred due to man's intervention? Only then can you recommend sound procedures for preserving these resources.

The material which follows is designed to assist you in this kind of learning process. By measuring and observing, for yourself, the physical, chemical and biological characteristics of a given area of the Bay, you can become more aware of the complexities of this ecosystem. This knowledge can be helpful in predicting the effects of various projects located on the Bay. It is sure to increase your awareness of environmental problems and give you some expertise in the discussion of these problems.

Whether your interests are broad environmental understanding, specific knowledge, pollution abatement, or simply the fun of investigating the area where you spend your recreational moments, we think this guide will prove an enjoyable and useful aid.

WATER STUDIES

The following list of suggested activities is provided as a guide. You may or may not wish to take data on all of these factors.

Date and Time. The importance of dating data collection in any scientific investigation cannot be overemphasized. By including a date and time with data collected, comparisons can be made over a period of time, i.e., hourly, daily, weekly, seasonally, etc. Inclusion of a date and time also permits one to readily go back and locate information from specific time in the past.

Depth of Reading. Whether a sample of water to be tested is taken at the surface, bottom, or somewhere in between is of utmost importance. Animal and plant life varies according to depth. The temperature, volume of dissolved gases such as CO_2 and O_2, salinity, and turbidity all vary according to depth. The amount of light penetration is governed by the depth and in this way affects the physical and biological characteristics of the sample under investigation. See instructions for lead-line construction.

H_2O Temp. Differences in H_2O temperature are caused by seasonal, daily, and hourly changes in atmospheric conditions (cloud cover, precipitation, air temperature, wind, etc.). In turn, animal and plant life, dissolved gases, and various chemical factors change according to temperature. Various plants and animals can tolerate wide differences in temperature, while others are killed off by a change of only a degree or two. The fact that the amount of dissolved gas varies with temperature is probably best evidenced by recalling the "pop" one hears in opening a warm bottle of soda compared with a refrigerated one. Cold water is able to hold more dissolved gases than warm water. An ordinary outdoor thermometer may be used to determine both the air and water temperature.

Salinity. Salts make up most of the dissolved minerals in water, particularly seawater. Ocean water contains about 3.5% or 35 ppt. (parts per thousand) dissolved minerals, while inland ponds and streams contain very minute quantities. Salinity in the Bay varies with depth, and proximity to the ocean and various fresh water tributaries. Most aquatic plants and animals cannot tolerate wide differences in salt content. To take a sand shark from the lower Bay region and transport it to the Susquehanna would surely kill it. The concentration of salts (salinity) in different areas in the Bay varies, and the native plant and animal life varies accordingly. Salinity is easily determined with a LaMotte salinity test kit.

Temperature and salinity follow three basic patterns in the Chesapeake Bay. In the period from March to August, warmer, fresher water flowing into the head of the Bay overlies colder, saltier water entering from the ocean; the months from September to December exhibit colder, fresher water overlying warmer saltier water; and the two winter months of January and February both demonstrate cold, fresh water overlying cold, salty water.

In the following table, temperature and salinity measured at a depth of 20 feet in mid-channel are recorded for three areas of the Chesapeake Bay at two-month intervals. Additional data for other locations, depths and times is available upon request. Figures were taken from the Chesapeake Bay Institute's report, "Temperature and Salinity Distributions in Vertical Sections Along the Longitudinal Axis of the Chesapeake Bay," September 1971.

Temperature (F°) at 20 ft., Mid-Channel

	January	March	May	July	September	November
Baltimore	35°	43°	57°	75°	74°	47°
Cedar Point (off Patuxent River)	36°	41°	58°	75°	74°	50°
Norfolk	38°	48°	59°	73°	72°	52°

Salinity (ppt.) at 20 ft., Mid-Channel

	January	March	May	July	September	November
Baltimore	15	14	10	8	15	11
Cedar Point	17	18	12	13	17	18
Norfolk	29	23	22	25	27	24

Dissolved Oxygen (D.O.). Oxygen-breathing organisms are referred to as aerobic, while non-oxygen-breathing organisms are called anerobic, e.g., tetanus bacteria which can only survive in deep, airless puncture wounds. The majority of organisms common to us breathe oxygen by various means, i.e., gills, lungs, absorption through the skin, etc. Even the green plants, which produce oxygen (O_2) through the process called photosynthesis, breathe in O_2 at night when a light source is no longer available. The amount of D.O. in a water sample varies according to temperature, presence and amount of animal and plant life, turbulence, depth of reading, etc. By collecting data on D.O. one can determine how well a community is balanced between green plants (oxygen producers) and animals (oxygen consumers). D.O. is most easily measured using a LaMotte dissolved oxygen test kit.

Acceptable dissolved O_2 levels have been set at not less than 4 ppm. (parts per million) in waters for general use and not less than 5.0 ppm. in areas used for the propagation of fish and other aquatic life, except in areas where lower levels occur naturally.

pH. pH is a measure of how acidic or how alkaline a water sample is, and is dependent on the concentration of hydrogen (H^+) ions; it is measured on a scale ranging from 1 to 14 with 7 representing neutrality. Hydrogen ions (H^+) and hydroxide ions (OH^-) are present in equilibrium in all water ($H^+ + OH^- = H_2O$). pH readings below 7 indicate a high concentration of (H^+) and an acid condition; the closer the pH is to 1, the more acid the sample. A pH above 7 means the solution has a higher concentration of (OH^-) than (H^+) and the solution is basic. As the pH approaches 14 the sample becomes severely basic. Most plants and animals exist within a certain pH range; an environment with a higher or lower pH is likely to cause death. Animals give off carbon dioxide during respiration. This reacts with water to form an acid. Therefore, a water sample with an acidic pH value may indicate an over-abundance of animals or a lack of green plants. Industrial effluents may also cause acid or basic conditions in various bodies of water. pH is easily measured with pH test paper, available at tropical fish supply stores or a LaMotte pH test kit. Normal pH values in the Chesapeake Bay range from 6.0 to 8.5.

It might be well to mention at this point that these tests do not just yield abstract figures. Salinity measurements of 15 ppt. indicate the ideal environment for oysters. Fish kills can result from low (less than 4 ppm.) dissolved oxygen levels. pH indicates the levels of plant and animal activity and imbalances of the two. An understanding of the effect of salinity, D.O., and pH levels on the ecological community can increase your appreciation of the complexity of the Bay environmental problems.

Turbidity. The amount of suspended particulate matter in a body of water is directly related to the turbidity or cloudiness of the sample. Suspended particles may result from nearby soil erosion, and from industrial, sanitary, and storm drainage systems emptying into the water system under study. Turbidity can also be caused by high concentrations of phytoplankton (microscopic plant life) which may result from the fertilizing effect of sewage effluents and agricultural runoff.

Suspended particles cause the sunlight hitting the water to be scattered or absorbed rather than penetrating to lower depths. Hence, depending on the amount of turbidity, many physical and biological factors can be affected. Turbidity is most readily measured with a Secchi Disk.

Types of Fish Noted. Fish can usually be observed from the shore or boat. Large quantities of various species can be caught using a seine (inexpensively purchased in local hobby or bait-tackle stores). Rather than identifying specific fish as to their species (although this is encouraged if time permits), identify their size, numbers, and depth at which they are found. Also, try to learn something about what they are feeding on, whether they feed at the surface, on the bottom, or both. If you wish to preserve your catch, make certain you take but one of each

species and return the remainder of your catch to the water im
mediately. Make sketches of those fish you wish to return to the wate
and want to identify at a later time. Pay particular attention to shape
fins, tail, and markings.

Types of Plant Life Noted. Plants can be roughly divided into thre
groups—submerged, emergent, and floating. Submerged and emergen
plants are generally rooted in the bottom with the submerged plant
being entirely covered by water and the emergent plants having under
water roots and a stem exposed to the air. Floating plants may or ma
not be rooted, but their mass is mostly on the surface. Plants can b
identified using one or more of the excellent identification books or
the market covering aquatic life (see identification book listing at th
back of this *Guide*). If such specific identification is undesirable, plant
can be grouped according to their size, relative numbers, location, anc
whether they are floating, emergent or submerged. Collected specimen
can be pressed between newspaper and weighted down to drive out th
moisture, or placed in a typical plant press. The finished product shoul
be labeled and mounted on white paper and covered with clear plasti
contact paper, available in most hardware stores.

Plankton. Plankton are microscopic plants (phytoplankton) and
microscopic animals (zooplankton) normally swimming or suspended ir
open water. These microscopic organisma represent the fundamenta
food for larger animals; what they lack in size they readily make up for
by their tremendous numbers. There are many fine identification books
which permit rapid classification. Interesting comparisons can be made
on where plankton are located in greatest abundance and at which time
of the day, year, etc. Simple identification may be made according to
whether the plankton is phytoplankton or zooplankton. Plankton nets
represent quite an expense if purchased through a scientific supply
house. A simple, inexpensive and readily constructed net may be made
by consulting the equipment construction sheet.

BEACH STUDIES

Zones of Study. It is important to realize that there are many regions
of a beach. The effect of the adjacent water on one region may closely
correspond or widely differ from the effects on another. Try to keep in
mind the relationships between these regions; how they are interdependent and how they work together in their ecosystem.

Spray Zone. This zone is constantly being sprayed by water (and
consequently salt) from wave action. Though this zone is practically
nonexistent in smaller tributaries, it extends much farther than it may
seem where waves occur. It may extend into bordering grasslands, dune
areas or the beginnings of a forest.

Intertidal Zone. This area is perhaps the most interesting region affected by the water for it is doused by tides twice a day. The length of time that each area within this zone is covered varies according to its elevation. When studying this zone note adaptions for breathing and eating. How does the submergent-emergent cycle affect the life of the plants and animals? Note whether tide is in or out. How can you determine this?

Submerged Zone. Though this zone might be considered better classified under water studies, it may also be studied here because this region has several characteristics similar to those on the beach. It is inhabited by tall plants whose roots are constantly underwater, but whose stems and leaves occasionally extend into the air. It is frequented by swans, herons, etc., adapted with long legs and necks.

Perhaps at the location which you are studying there is no beach, but cliffs which drop swiftly at the water's edge. When trying to gain an overall viewpoint of the water, think of the effects of such a formation. Consider the fact that there are no grasses growing here, no shelter for small fish and no wave action to help provide dissolved oxygen. Whichever kind of border is formed at the water's edge, note what materials it is composed of (silt, sand, clay, earth, rock). How and to what extent does this material provide nutrients for life?

Equipment. There are many tools which can be used when conducting your beach studies. Though observation by means of your various senses is undoubtedly of the highest importance, the use of these tools can be quite helpful. Binoculars can be quite helpful to identify birds. Use a sieve to extract organisms from the wet mud or sand. A seine net can be used to investigate the shallows. Trot lines and crab nets can be used to find the presence of crabs in the water farther out. Devise your own equipment to investigate the waters. Refer to our test equipment instruction sheets for more information.

Animals and Plants. Note and identify as many as possible. Don't forget the birds. How does each one interrelate with its environment? Where does each fit in a food chain? Look for adaptations such as mouths, feet, roots, etc., which enable each plant and animal to live more easily in its niche. How do the plants and animals that you observe depend upon each other, the water, land, air, beach? What would be the effect on each should the water become covered with ¼ inch of *oil?*

Man. Is the water you are studying being used commercially? Has man changed it by dredging, clamming, crabbing, etc.? Has it been changed by developing its shores; destroying natural marshes? Is there foreign matter (litter) in the water? Have you seen anything discharged into the water? Are there any indications (dead fish, birds, or plants) of pollution? How is man affecting this natural area, this part of our Bay? How are you affecting the Bay?

MARSHES

More and more we are finding that marshes are both interesting and important. They are natural sediment traps—this means that they tend to be much more stable than beaches. But, even more important, they trap nutrient-rich sediments suspended in slowly flowing water. Thus, marsh soil is fertile. It is not, however, an easy place for plants to live. They must withstand high concentrations of salt; also they must withstand having their roots alternately flooded and dried out as the tide rises and falls. In a rigorous situation like this, it is common to find that a few species do very well. They are present in large numbers, while other species are rare. This is true of the Chesapeake's salt marshes. They are dominated by grasses of the genus *Spartina,* especially *Spartina alterniflora,* which is tall and coarse and grows where it is flooded twice a day by the tides; and *Spartina patens,* salt hay grass, which is shorter and finer and grows higher on the marsh where it is flooded less often.

The *Spartina* grasses are the dominant plants on the marshes. Thus they are the base of the marsh food web—they provide the food for the marsh community, but very few of the marsh animals eat marsh grass directly. Instead, the system is based on detritus, a mixture of partially decayed marsh grass and decay bacteria. Marsh grasses have tough, indigestible outer coverings, but bacteria can break them down after the grass dies. This decaying grass adds to the fertility of the marsh soil for future generations of *Spartina.* But it also adds to the fertility of the water. These bits and scraps of digested grass provide food for a variety of animals that live in the waterways of the marsh. Some, like clams, oysters, periwinkle, and microscopic animals, eat the detritus directly. Others, like crabs, juvenile fish, and some adult fish, eat the animals which feed on the detritus.

Beyond directly providing habitat and food, marshes contribute some of their accumulated dead organic material to surrounding deeper waters. This material furnishes food for filter feeders like oysters, and nutrients for microscopic plants (phytoplankton) upon which food webs are primarily based. Thus the contribution of marshes to a large body of water is substantial.

Incidentally, it is worth noting here that the very success of the *Spartina* grasses implies instability in the marsh food web. A web based on only one or two species of plant can collapse if anything destroys the marsh as a habitat for those species. Pollution or draining of a marsh can ruin its stands of *Spartina.*

There are some larger animals that live and feed either part- or full-time on the marshes. The most common mammals are the raccoon, that feeds primarily on clams and fiddler crabs, and the muskrat, that feeds on roots and makes lodges of the stems of the marsh grasses. Others, rarer and more retiring, include mink, otter, and, if the marsh is large or close to woods, white-tailed deer. Among the birds, the fish-eating herons are most common. They include the great blue heron, the smaller green heron, and the American egret. Other fish-eating birds are kingfishers, ospreys, and a few bald eagles, as well as small shorebirds like sandpipers.

The most useful tools for observing a marsh are, again, the senses. Walk a marsh, or move through it slowly and quietly in a boat. Look and listen. As you move, look into the water and at the edge of the bank. Look around the base of the grasses and anywhere else where there is shade for small animals in the summer. On open patches of sand or mud, look for tracks of mammals and birds. Take a pair of binoculars and a book like *A Field Guide to the Birds* and try to identify the birds you see. But remember to watch them and their activities too. Identifying is not the same thing as observing. Low tide is a good time to look at a marsh. Much is visible then that is not visible later. Sunrise and sunset are also good times to be around. Mammals especially do not spend much time actively on the marshes during the day. Try also to visit a marsh at different seasons of the year.

Other techniques besides walking and looking are useful. In shallow water mudflats, look for small round holes. These are siphon holes for clams. If you like, try to dig with one hand down into the hold to catch the clam. But dig fast—clams can burrow very well; and be prepared to get yourself wet. Buy a minnow seine from a sporting goods store and pull it in shallow marsh lagoons. Crabs, juvenile fish, killifish—it is always amazing what turns up in a seine. Run some chemical water tests too. Because of decaying materials and summer sun warming shallow water, dissolved oxygen levels get low sometimes, but the flushing action of the tides tends to minimize this.

Finally, look at the transition areas where the marshland gets higher and therefore flooded less often by the tides. Conditions in these areas are less rigorous for plants, so there is more diversity. These areas are interesting as they change from marshland to upland and woods.

Foraging. Marshes that are fertile ground for so many food finfish and shellfish are also good for the person who enjoys foraging wild foods. Clams, mussels, oysters, crabs, and perwinkles are abundant, as are some edible marsh border plants like orach, sea rocket, and sheep sorrel. Foraging is a profound way for man to relate to his environment.

While you are in the mood to forage, remember crabs and larger fish. Some directions for crabbing are included later in this *Guide,* in case you are not already experienced as an amateur crabber. Fishing is a large topic. If you have no experience at it, your best bet is to check with a local sporting goods store. Probably the easiest way to get started is to rig a handline with a sinker at the bottom and two hooks, 6 and 12 inches above the sinker. Bait the hooks with bits of bloodworm or peeler crab and fish over areas where the bottom is hard sand, preferably 10—25 ft. deep. Fish with the sinker on the bottom and the line tight above it. Set the hook with a snap of the wrist when a fish bites. Trout and spot, and less frequently, croakers, rockfish, and blue-fish can be caught in this way. All are fine for eating. Another technique that will sometimes take blues and rock in the summer and early fall is to trail a handline from a sailboat. This is called trolling and should be done with a bucktail or metal spoon as a lure. It is most productive in areas where the fish are feeding on the surface, usually on schools of marsh-bred shiners (silversides). Such areas are marked by gulls feeding on scraps left behind by the fish. By the way, if you catch a blue, beware of his sharp teeth—a caught blue is not above snapping at his captor.

Again, remember that the foregoing instructions are minimal. Seek advice from tackle dealers, marina operators, and fishermen. Many will be glad to help get you started.

Two other notes about marshes and their environs. Look at birds and at the trees in the uplands beyond the marsh. Many species of birds call the Bay home or highway at different seasons of the year. One particularly enjoyable time to watch them is summer; ospreys, herons, and their kin have been mentioned. In fresher water marshes, the male redwing blackbird is conspicuous. Another time is late fall, winter, and early spring. The Bay also harbors several species of attractive or amusing ducks, including mallards, teal, canvasbacks, redheads, mergansers, buffleheads, ruddy ducks, and old squaws. Even more spectacular are Canada geese and whistling swans.

INSTRUCTION SHEETS FOR WATER
TEST EQUIPMENT

Secchi Disk. Lower in the water until it can no longer be seen. If there is glare, try looking at it from different angles. Record the level at which it disappears. Lower it another 1–2 ft. and begin raising it slowly. Record the level at which it reappears. Add the two readings and divide the sum by 2 to get the average turbidity for that spot. Readings of 4' to 8' are most common.

Sample Bottle #1. (For samples near surface only.) Place bottle just above surface of water. Quickly lower it to a 1–2' depth and hold it there until air bubbles stop surfacing. This will give a sample with most of the water from the depth of the *top* of the bottle when submerged.

1.

2.

Sample Bottle #2. (For samples from a specific depth.) This is the same as #1 except that it has a cork in the hole with a string attached. The cork should be placed in the hole with only a little bit of pressure. Under water you may not be able to release the cork if it fits tightly because of the inward pressure of the water. Lower the bottle to the desired depth and give the string (to cork) a sudden jerk. This will release the cork if it is not too tight and the lines are clear. Often the corkstring and line to the bottle will get tangled. It may help to use a heavier weight and have the two lines farther apart at the surface. To obtain an accurate temperature reading leave the bottle, filled with water, at the desired depth for 10–15 minutes.

Plankton Net. Make sure that all lines are fastened very securely. Tow slowly through water so as not to put too much pressure on the net. The faster you go the more plankton you collect but if you go too fast you could possibly lose the rig. By dragging the net slowly or by attaching weights, deep-water plankton collections may be made.

Test Kits. We highly recommend that a layer of newspapers be placed under the kits during use to protect the surface under them. Some of the chemicals in use will leave permanent stains on a surface—even on fiberglass.

General Test Kit Instructions
Loading a Syringe (see illustrations)

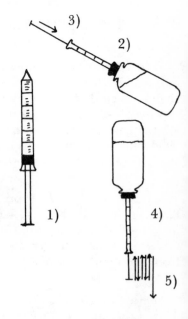

1) Pull out the plunger most of the way to fill the syringe with air.
2) Insert syringe into the fitting on the cap of the bottle.
3) Press plunger in all the way to push the air into the bottle.
4) Invert bottle. Then pull plunger about ½ way out and push back about 3 times rapidly. This should get any air bubbles out of the syringe. If it doesn't then try tapping the syringe to make them rise. Then try pulling it in and out again.
5) Pull syringe plunger out to last mark.

Titrating. Carefully add the titrant drop by drop to the solution. Between each drop mix the solution thoroughly. To compare the color be sure and use a consistently colored white background. When the solution suddenly changes you have reached the "end point."

Dissolved Oxygen Test Kit. Follow instructions *very* carefully. It is better to read the directions and then reread them step by step as you do them. Be sure that your glassware (sample bottle, syringe, burrette, etc.) is very clean. If possible, scrub and rinse thoroughly with distilled water. To get a better reading, rinse out the sample bottle with part of the sample first, then fill it until it overflows. When adding the acid you may need to add a little extra to get the precipitate (solid parts formed in sample) to dissolve. When adding more than one burretteful of titrant (sodium thiosulfate) be sure to push the burrette to "20" only; do not go to the end. Also be sure to carefully note how many times you refill the burrette and don't forget to add both amounts (before and after iodine is added) of sodium thiosulfate to figure your ppm. (parts per million).

Salinity Test Kit. Be *extremely* careful with this kit. One of the chemicals is silver nitrate which stains very badly and cannot be removed from decks. Remember in this kit to use the red-lettered syringe for adding the sample and the black-lettered one for adding the titrant. Also remember to use distilled water in the titration tube and add .5 cc. of the sample.

pH Test Kit. Fill one tube to the line with the sample. Remember: the closer to the line you are, the more accurate your reading. If you look carefully at the surface of the water you will see a curve called a miniscus. Be sure and use the *bottom* of this curve and *not the top*.

Carefully add 10 drops of pH indicator. After mixing, place test tube in one hole in the top of the comparator. Find the closest color. You may have to put it into the other hole to get it between the right colors. You can give your readings with more accuracy by guessing how much difference there is between the colors. This will enable you to get readings like 7.6 and 8.3.

Seine. A minnow seine can be bought in a good hardware or sporting goods store for $2, but you'll have to get some poles (mop handles are perfect). Drag the seine (weights down/floats up) along the bottom in a shallow area up onto a beach. You must have two people working it. Keep the bottoms of the poles about one foot ahead of the tops so that the poles lean backwards. Make sure that the weights drag along the bottom but also try to keep the floats near the surface. In other words—ideally the water should be a little shallower than the width of the net.

Crabbing

Crablines. Take some cotton string in lengths about 1½ to twice the depth of the water and tie one end to a piece of crab bait and the other end to a boat or dock. Toss the baited end away from you out into the water and let it rest on the bottom for 5–10 minutes. Pull it in *very* slowly and steadily; *no* sudden jerks. Pull the crab (if you have caught one) as close to the surface as you can and scoop it quickly.

Trotline. Two people in an ordinary dinghy can manage a trotline without difficulty. One rows along the line slowly and quietly. The other does the dipping. Dip with decision, and deftly. Blue crabs hanging onto chicken necks are fortunately careless of their lives, but they can be disturbed by clumsy dipping. The line should be drawn over the bow, or an oar, without jerks or any other sudden moves. In the prime times—early morning and late afternoon—the line can be frequently worked. Remember to set the floats and anchors to take advantage of the tide, and be sure to allow the bait to rest on the bottom. Crabs caught in this fashion come out fighting mad. They can be dumped into the bottom of the dinghy, but not when bare toes are exposed.

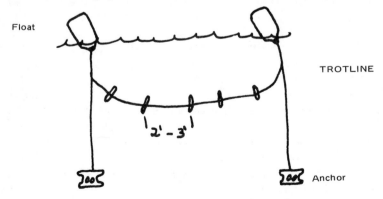

Float

TROTLINE

2' – 3'

Anchor

Crab Bait. Fish heads, chicken necks (actually any chicken parts) or pieces of salted eel may be used for bait.

Ring Nets; Crab Pots. A notably peculiar characteristic of the Bay region is the way in which local custom and tradition have developed different techniques for harvesting seafood. Crab pots predominate in the lower Bay; trotlines in the upper Bay. Strangely, the ring net is seldom used.

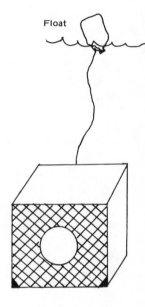

CRAB POT

The ring net is ideal for yachtsmen because it is easy to stow. It consists of a ring of wood or metal from 2' to 3' in diameter, to which is attached a shallow net, 1' to 2' in depth. To use, simply attach crab bait to the center of the net and lower to the bottom. A three-line halter is attached to the ring. In lively waters, raise the net after it has rested on the bottom about 15 minutes. It is not unusual to catch as many as 4 or 5 crabs at a time. The renowned forager, Euell Gibbons, advises us that a ring net often produces an entire meal for a couple of hearty eaters from a single haul.

Crab pots are wire cages usually used with a float to mark the spot where they have been dropped. Too large to take on most pleasure boats, they are best worked by those who have easy access to the water with small boats.

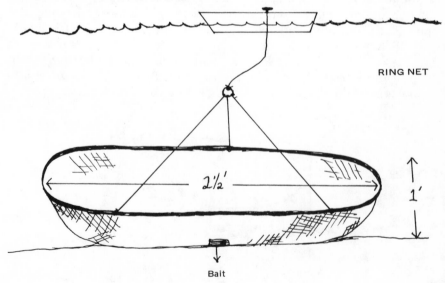

RING NET

2½'

1'

Bait

INSTRUCTIONS FOR FABRICATING ECOLOGICAL
STUDY EQUIPMENT

SECCHI DISK

May be cut from metal sheeting or exterior plywood. Disk should be 9" (20 cm.) in diameter and painted white. A screw eye or hook should be fastened in the center for attaching a line. Lower disk in water until it disappears. Lower more and then raise until it reappears. Average the two readings to find TURBIDITY.

Line marked
every 10 cm.
or 6 inches.

Weight can
be added if   →
necessary

SOUNDING LINE
(used for measuring the depth of the water)

Line marked every
10 cm. or 6 inches.
Make special marks
every meter or yard.

Weight fastened securely

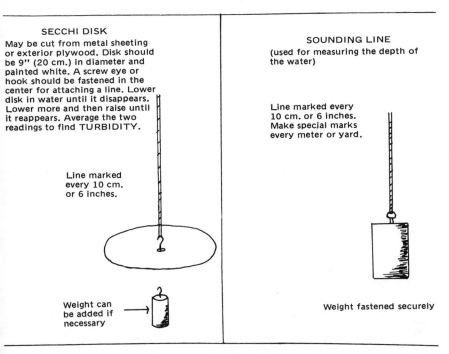

SIEVE
(strainer)

Take along a kitchen sieve to filter organizms from mud. Many mud or sand shores are suitable habitats for worms and snails.

GRAPPLING BAR

Used for pulling rooted plants from the bottom to the surface for examination. Attach to a line about 25 feet long.

Metal Bar or Pipe

10-penny nails

Towropes

After securely fastening the end of the line to your waist or the boat, throw the bar far out into the water. Drag it back toward you slowly.

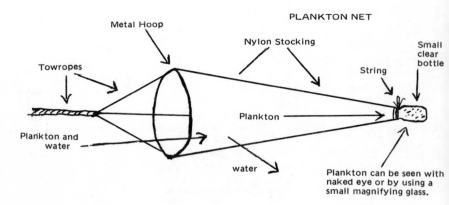

PLANKTON NET

Metal Hoop

Nylon Stocking

Small clear bottle

Towropes

String

Plankton

Plankton and water

water

Plankton can be seen with naked eye or by using a small magnifying glass.

EPILOGUE

The experiments you conduct are related to the following conditions, each of which has a significant bearing on the health of Bay waters.

(1) Eutrophication (excessive enrichment causing dissolved oxygen depletion).
   Turbidity, dissolved oxygen, pH.
(2) Industrial pollution (thermal, chemical, oil from plant and storm drainage).
   Temperature, water samples.
(3) Agricultural runoff (pesticides and herbicides and inorganic fertilizers).
   Dissolved oxygen.
(4) Fish kills (oxygen depletion, acidity, weather).
   pH.
(5) Algae blooms.
   Secchi disk, pH, dissolved oxygen.
(6) Microscopic animal and plant productivity.
   Plankton net.
(7) Bird and fish life.
   Binoculars, seine nets, trotlines, etc.
(8) Plant life.
   Grappling hooks, spade.
(9) Turbidity (cloudiness).
   Secchi disk and plankton nets.
(10) Shore development, Bay population.
   Observation and all tools.

Good Luck!

RESOURCE MATERIAL

Useful Handbooks for Identification of Bay and Shore Life

Chamberlain, Charles J., *Gymnosperms,* 1966; Dover Publications Inc., New York

Ditmars, Raymond L., *The Reptiles of North America,* 1936; Doubleday & Co., New York

Golden Nature Guide Series, Golden Press, New York
 Birds of North America, Chandler S. Robbins
 Fishes, A Guide to Fresh and Salt-water Species, Zim and Shoemaker
 Flowers, Zim and Martin
 Insects, Zim and Cottam
 Pond Life, Reid and Zim
 Seashores, A Guide to Animals and Plants Along the Beaches, Zim and Ingle
 Trees, Zim and Martin

Griffith, Ruth, *Phytoplankton of the Chesapeake Bay,* Chesapeake Biological Lab., Solomons, Md.

Keeler, Harriett, *Our Northern Shrubs,* 1969; Dover Publications Inc., New York

Needham, J.G. and P.R., *A Guide to the Study of Fresh-Water Biology,* 1962; Holden Day Inc., San Francisco, Ca.

The Peterson Field Guide Series, Houghton Mifflin Company, Boston, Ma.
 A Field Guide to the Animal Tracks, Olaus J. Murie
 A Field Guide to the Birds, Roger Tory Peterson
 A Field Guide to the Ferns, Boughton Cobb
 A Field Guide to the Insects, Borror and White
 A Field Guide to the Mammals, Bart and Grossenheider
 A Field Guide to the Reptiles and Amphibians, Roger Conant
 A Field Guide to the Rocks and Minerals, Frederick H. Pough
 A Field Guide to the Shells (Atlantic and Gulf Coasts), Percy A. Morris
 A Field Guide to the Shrubs, George A. Petrides
 A Field Guide to the Wildflowers, Peterson and McKenny

Picture-Keyed Nature Series, William C. Brown Company, Dubuque, Ia.
 How to Know the Freshwater Algae, G.W. Prescott
 How to Know the Freshwater Fishes, Samuel Eddy

Putnam's Nature Field Books, G.P. Putnam and Sons, New York
 Field Book of American Wildflowers, F. Schuyler Mathews

Putnam's Nature Field Books (*cont.*)
  The New Field Book of Fresh Water Life, Elsie B. Klots
  Field Book of Insects, Frank E. Lutz
  Field Book of Marine Fishes of the Atlantic Coast, Charles M.
    Breder, Jr.
  Field Book of Nature Activities and Hobbies, William Hillcourt
  Field Book of Ponds and Streams, Ann Haven Morgan
  Field Book of Reptiles and Amphibians, Cochran and Goin
  Field Book of Trees and Shrubs, F. Schuyler Mathews
Sargent, Charles S., *Manual of the Trees of North America (Volumes 1 and 2),* 1922; Dover Publications Inc., New York
The Tilton School Water Pollution Program, *Water Pollution and Environmental Studies,* Environmental Protection Agency
Ward and Whipple, *Fresh Water Biology,* John Wiley & Sons, Inc., New York

Suggested Reading Materials

Bridges, William, *The New York Aquarium Book of the Water World,* 1970; American Heritage Press, New York
Commoner, Barry, *The Closing Circle,* Alfred A. Knopf, Inc., New York
Eckert, Allan W., *Wild Season,* 1967; Little-Brown & Co., Boston, Ma.
Gibbons, Euell Theophilus, *Stalking the Blue-Eyed Scallop,* 1964; David McKay Co. Inc., New York
Henderson, Richard and Bartlett Dunbar, *Sail & Power,* 1967; U.S. Naval Institute, Annapolis, Md.
Klingel, Gilbert C., *The Bay,* 1967; Dodd, Mead & Co., New York

Bibliography

Blair, C.H., and W.D. Ansel, *Chesapeake Bay: Notes and Sketches,* 1970; Tidewater Publishers, Cambridge, Md.
Gibbons, Euell Theophilus, *Stalking the Blue-Eyed Scallop,* 1964; David McKay Co. Inc., New York
Klingel, Gilbert C., *The Bay,* 1967; Dodd, Mead & Co., New York
Peterson, R.T., *A Field Guide to the Birds,* 1947; Houghton Mifflin Co., New York
Shurtleff, B.P. and G.C. Klingel, *Seeing Chesapeake Wilds,* 1971; International Marine Publishing Co., Camden, Me.
Teal, J. and M., *Life and Death of the Salt Marsh,* 1969; National Audubon Society, Ballantine Books, New York
Wass, M.L. and T.D. Wright, *Coastal Wetlands of Virginia: Interim Report of the Governor and General Assembly,* 1969; Special Report #10 of the Virginia Institute of Marine Science

GLOSSARY OF TERMS

adjacent—near or close to something; neighboring

aerobic—able to live or grow only where oxygen is present

algae bloom—an over-production of algae usually caused by fertilization of the water

anaerobic—able to live and grow where there is no air or free oxygen

aquatic—growing or living in or upon water

benthic—relating to, or occurring at the bottom of a body of water

burrette—a graduated (marked) tube used for measuring small quantities of liquid or gas

CO_2 (carbon dioxide)—a colorless, odorless gas, somewhat heavier than air that is exhaled from the lungs of animals and absorbed by plants

cm. (centimeter)—a unit of measurement in the metric system meaning one one-hundredth of a meter

cc. (cubic centimeter)—a unit of volume measurement in the metric system equal to one one-thousandth of a liter

dinghy—a small boat used as a tender to a yacht or sailboat

dissolved minerals—minerals which have liquified or merged into a solution

distilled water—purified water that has had all dissolved minerals removed from it

D.O. (dissolved oxygen)—oxygen which has merged into water and is most readily available to water-breathing organisms

diurnal—having a daily cycle

ecosystem—the relationship between the physical environment and the community of living organisms for a specific location

effluent—flowing out or forth such as the outflow of a sewer or sewage tank

e.g.—(L. *exempli gratia*) for the sake of example; for example

emergent—an outgrowth from beneath

end point—that point in a chemical reaction where a given amount of one substance completely reacts with an unknown amount of another substance; usually made visible by the use of liquid indicators which change colors when the end point is reached

engulf—to swallow up; overwhelm

equilibrium—a state of balance or equality

erosion—wearing away gradually; disintegration

estuary—an inlet or arm of the sea where the tide and salt water meet the freshwater currents from the draining land

eutrophication—overenrichment of nutrients in a water body causing an algae bloom; as the algae die from overcrowding and a lack of sunlight, the water becomes stagnant from a lack of oxygen

food chain—the step-by-step progression of one organism depending on the next for food; example: grass → cow → human

forager—a person who searches for his own food or provisions in the wild

herbicide—a chemical used to kill plants

H_2O—chemical symbol for water

i.e.—(L. *id est*) that is

interdependent—one organism depending on another and vice versa; both organisms depending on each other

intertidal zone—the zone of a beach which is alternately covered and uncovered by water as the tide rises and falls

ion—an electrically charged atom or group of atoms; the electrical charge that results when a neutral atom or group of atoms loses or gains one or more electrons (negative charges surrounding the nucleus)

liter—basic unit of volume in the metric system; slightly more than one quart

longitudinal—running lengthwise

miniscus—horizontal upper surface or boundary of any liquid in a container; one should always read the bottom of this horizontal bubble

mg/l—milligrams per liter, measurement of weight per volume

niche—a way of life (in ecology); an organism's way of life or "occupation"; the sum of all the relationships between any species of organism and its environment

non-point source—originating from many locations with no clearly defined source, such as land runoff

O_2—oxygen gas

photosynthesis—the process by which green plants use light to form carbohydrates from water and carbon dioxide

plankton—microscopic animal and plant life found floating or drifting in the ocean or fresh water, used as food by fish

point-source—originating from one identifiable and highly localized source, such as an industrial effluent pipe

pollution—contamination or alteration that impairs the legitimate beneficial use of such land or water and may endanger wildlife or man

ppm.—parts per million

ppt.—parts per thousand

propagation—to reproduce itself; raise or breed

proximity—nearness in space, time, etc.

respiration—process of breathing; inhaling and exhaling air

salinity—the quality or degree of being saline; salty; saltiness seine—a large fishing net with floats along the top edge and weights along the bottom

sieve—a utensil having many small meshed openings of a size allowing passage only to liquids or to finer particles of loose matter; sifter; strainer

sounding line—a line or cable weighted at one end and used for measuring the depth of water

submerged—under water

tetanus—lockjaw; an acute infectious disease caused by the toxins given off by non-air-breathing bacteria

titration—the process of finding out how much of a certain substance is contained in a solution by measuring how much of another substance must be added to the solution in order to produce a given reaction

titrant—the substance of known strength which is being added to the unknown solution

trotline—a strong line suspended from distant floats, with short, baited lines hung from it at intervals; trawl line

turbulence—agitation; disturbance; disorder

vertical—upright relative to the horizon; straight up and down

> —greater than

< —lesser than